DANGER PAY

Focus on American History Series
Center for American History
University of Texas at Austin
EDITED BY DON CARLETON

Danger Pay

MEMOIR OF A PHOTOJOURNALIST
IN THE MIDDLE EAST,
1984–1994

BY CAROL SPENCER MITCHELL
EDITED BY ELLEN SPENCER SUSMAN

UNIVERSITY OF TEXAS PRESS, AUSTIN

Requests for permission to reproduce material from this work should be sent to:
Permissions
University of Texas Press
P.O. Box 7819
Austin, TX 78713-7819
www.utexas.edu/utpress/about/bpermission.html

⊗ The paper used in this book meets the minimum requirements of ANSI/NISO Z39.48-1992 (R1997) (Permanence of Paper).

LIBRARY OF CONGRESS CATALOGING-IN-PUBLICATION DATA

Mitchell, Carol Spencer, 1954–2004.
    Danger pay : memoir of a photojournalist in the Middle East, 1984–1994 / by Carol Spencer Mitchell ; edited by Ellen Spencer Susman. — 1st ed.
        p.   cm. — (Focus on American history series)
    ISBN 978-0-292-71882-1 (cloth : alk. paper)
    1. Arab countries—Description and travel. 2. Arab countries—Pictorial works. 3. Mitchell, Carol Spencer, 1954–2004. 4. Photojournalists—United States—Biography. I. Susman, Ellen Spencer, 1950– II. Title.
    DS36.65.M58   2008
    956.05'3092—dc22   2008012869
    [B]

DANGER PAY

A journalistic term for a special fee
photographers are paid
when working in a war zone.

To Carol
and all the journalists
who risk their lives
to bring us the truth.

————

To Carol's husband, Brian,
and their son, Sam—
the loves of her life.

Contents

Foreword

"People say that images speak for themselves," the late Carol Spencer Mitchell states near the end of her intensely thoughtful memoir. "They take for granted that the camera can reveal something that one person saw and another did not; that a picture doesn't lie. They forget that when a photographer creates an image, the flow of time passing has been arrested." Spencer Mitchell's troubled observation reveals the inner struggle that she and many of her fellow photojournalists experience while they work to provide fresh news images for the mass media. At the heart of her concern was the fear that she was an active participant in a process that was resulting in "the triumph of image over reality."

This deeply felt worry about the nature and meaning of her work serves as the underlying theme of Carol Spencer Mitchell's engrossing memoir, *Danger Pay*. Her well-stated expressions of doubt about the use and misuse of news photography, her observations about the morally complex nature of the Israeli-Palestinian dispute, and her fascinating descriptions of her meetings with Jordan's King Hussein and the PLO's Yasser Arafat are among several reasons why *Danger Pay* deserves a wide audience.

As director of the Center for American History and editor of the Focus on American History series at the University of Texas Press, I am especially pleased that the Center has sponsored the publication of this outstanding memoir. The Center, which has assembled a nationally important archive documenting this history of American photojournalism, serves as the permanent home for the Carol Spencer Collection. Consisting of approximately 60,000 photographs dating from 1977 until the early 1990s, this historically valuable collection includes images that Spencer Mitchell took as a photojournalist on special assignment for *Time, Newsweek, U.S. News &*

World Report, the *Washington Post*, the *Los Angeles Times*, and other news publications in the United States and Europe. The Spencer Collection, which includes the manuscript for this memoir and others of her papers, features her photographic work in the United States, the Caribbean, Central and South America, the Middle East, and North Africa. Of special interest are her photographs of United Nations Ambassador Andrew Young, the state visits to Washington by such dignitaries as Prime Minister Menachem Begin of Israel and President Anwar Sadat of Egypt in 1978, and Pope John Paul II's stop in Philadelphia in 1979. Spencer Mitchell worked in the Middle East prior to her move to Jerusalem in 1984. Some of her images are among the most powerful ever taken of the bleak border area between Israel, Lebanon, and Syria.

While still managing to cover various state visits and politicians as well as events such as the hijacking of the *Achille Lauro* in 1985, Spencer Mitchell was most drawn to the suffering she found in the refugee and PLO camps of the Gaza Strip and Lebanon before, during, and after the intifada of the 1980s. Her archive also includes extensive visual documentation of many key players in the Middle East conflict in the 1980s and 1990s. An inventory of the Carol Spencer Collection can be found on the Internet at http://www.lib.utexas.edu/taro/utcah/00542/cah-00542.html.

Carol Spencer married Brian Mitchell, a United Nations official, in 1994. Ten years later, she died of breast cancer at the age of fifty. Since Spencer Mitchell's death, her sister, Ellen Spencer Susman, has presented her writings and photographs to audiences across the country as testimony to the fact that the violence Carol Spencer Mitchell witnessed in the Middle East continues to have repercussions today. Ellen Susman, a talented media professional in her own right, deserves our recognition and sincere gratitude not only for donating the Carol Spencer Collection to the Center for American History but also for her persistent efforts to make the publication of *Danger Pay* possible.

DON CARLETON
Executive Director
Center for American History
University of Texas at Austin

Acknowledgments

Sorting through Carol's voluminous notes and photographs to produce *Danger Pay* was a daunting task. When Brian sent me a suitcase crammed full of slides, plus six banker's boxes of written material, it became obvious that I needed help. Fortunately, at every stage of this lengthy process, the right person appeared on the scene. My sincere thanks to the following:

Ann Tucker, the Houston Museum of Fine Arts esteemed Curator of Photography, found graduate student Elena John to organize Carol's immense collection of slides and photographs. Ann's advice was invaluable; Elena's work was impeccable.

Judy Little sorted through thousands of pages and synchronized numerous edits to put *Danger Pay* together.

Margaret Miller coordinated the written and visual materials I use when presenting my sister's work.

Wendy Watkins, who invited me to present Carol's work at Houston Photofest 2006.

Don Carleton, for his vision and advocacy of *Danger Pay*.

Holly Taylor, who guided me through the "final" edits to bring *Danger Pay* to life!

And finally, to Mom, Dad, Susan, and Steve—who believed I could get it done.   ELLEN SPENCER SUSMAN

DANGER PAY

Prologue

Everything has changed, they say, since that day. September 11, 2001.

She is a photographer. For seventeen years she lived in the Middle East, where terror was commonplace and everyday. Now, back in the USA, her nightmare is that the violence she witnessed through the camera's lens is still with her, tethered in the shadows of her darkroom.

"Remember that cover you took for *Newsweek* back in 1986?" her dad asks over the telephone. "The one that says, 'America Is Our Target.'"

"You mean for the story on terrorism in the Middle East?"

"I'm looking at it now." He reads aloud, "'Inside the Terror Network . . .' You know that same cover could be used today," he muses. She hasn't looked at it in years. "You should use it on the cover of the book you're writing."

She suddenly realizes he's on to something.

"And finish telling your story," he says quietly.

She snaps the door shut so no one will intrude. Acids cut through weariness, flood the brain, linger on her hands, her hair, her clothes. She lays some film down on the counter, allows herself time to recall everything. In the amber glow of this inner space no one barges in.

Make me a print.

Okay.

In the darkness she stands at the enlarger: shoulders curved, eyes looking down as clear, white light streams through the negative, projecting an image onto a sheet of smooth-white, semi-matte paper. She pulls the scene into focus, gazing at life as she once saw it, an isolated moment she tried to possess. The greasy thing about time, she thinks, is that it never lets what is be.

She slides the paper into a tray that she rocks gently so developer can swim evenly across the ivory rectangle. Three vertical streaks at the top come up first, a roundish smudge beneath, and just to the right, another thin line. Dark shapes become the sleek barrel of a PK machine gun. Next, the outline of a young man floats on the wet paper. His thick black turban surfaces fast, followed by his curly brown mustache and beard, then his olive-drab jacket appears, and a space where his face should be. Finally she sees the copper-toned rounds of belted ammunition, draped casually around his shoulders.

She studies his face as it materializes on the page. Wonders why this particular image was the one *Newsweek*'s editors decided to use to illustrate a cover story headlined "America Is Our Target: Inside the Terror Network" (April 7, 1986). She wonders, too, if the young Palestinian fighter, who she photographed in Lebanon, managed to stay alive after his portrait was published.

What her editors didn't realize is that they chose the wrong picture. Despite her captions, they identified "the terrorist" as the young bearded man. The image they should have shown is the one she is developing now—the group of six- and seven-year-olds in camouflaged battle fatigues, carrying Soviet-made AK-47s, marching in formation. These children, each of whom wears a dog tag containing a picture of a brother or a father, a sister or an uncle who died when their refugee homes were strafed by bombs. They are the ones we have to worry about. The young girls and boys who have learned to kill and who want to die in a suicide mission. Where will they be in seventeen years' time?

That is now . . .

She pulls the photograph out and drops it into the next tray to stop it developing further. She frowns, remembering the moment of the picture. News, she thinks, fact and fiction. She leans over the sink, then moves the picture to a third tray of acid that will fix the image.

Is it done?
Yes.
Show me.

[2]

PART 1

There's a New Kid in Town

LOCATION/YEAR: NEW YORK, ISRAEL,
JORDAN; 1984, 1985

A photograph is not just
the result of an encounter
between an event and a
photographer; picture-taking is
an event in itself.
—SUSAN SONTAG

The thing that's important
to know is that you never
know. You're always
sort of feeling your way.
—DIANE ARBUS

1

The Burning Bush

(OCTOBER 1984)

Why Israel?

It was a question that would haunt me throughout my stay in the Middle East. First my father, later my mother. In between the professionals and colleagues.

"You're going where?" my father says over the telephone.

"Israel."

"For how long?" I can tell by his tone that he's not pleased.

"I'm not sure," I reply. "A few months, maybe longer. I was hoping we could have dinner before I leave."

"Where are you now?"

"New York."

"I know you don't want to hear this, but I don't think this is a particularly wise move. What you really ought to do is get a normal nine-to-five job, learn how to dress properly, live in the real world for a change, stop acting like a gypsy. You know you did just turn thirty."

"Yes, I'm aware of that, Dad. But I'm scheduled to fly out next week. Besides, I'm looking forward to spending some time there. And I've already sublet my apartment."

"Well, where will you be staying?"

"Jerusalem."

"What's the name of the hotel?"

"I don't know yet . . ."

Our conversation is nothing new, a minor variation on a familiar theme. Adventure—which includes anything that might come under the heading of diversity or change—is perceived by my father as negative deviation, a reckless departure from permanence and stability. That one can gather bits and pieces of moveable life together and simply depart baffles him.

". . . I promise, it's perfectly safe."

"It's foolish. How are you planning to support yourself?"

"I'll get assignments . . . and freelance."

I hear a long sigh, silence, then finally, "Why do you want to go to Israel?"

It's a question I've pondered myself. I'm not sure whether or not I'll be able to make a living. I have a few assignments, enough to keep me going for several months. I'll have to cope with the competition between journalists and collect visas. I have no friends there to speak of.

I've traveled to other Middle Eastern countries in the last few years. In 1982, I was on assignment for *Time* magazine to cover daily life in the West Bank and the Gaza Strip. I returned again for *Time* in 1984 to photograph Libya's Muammar Qadhafi. But this is different. I'm moving in, resettling.

Then there is my own history: assimilated Jew. My grandfather changed his name. I've never been to a synagogue, have no Jewish friends, didn't even really know any Jews until I moved to New York. I knew I was "Jewish," but it meant nothing to me, was not a topic of conversation. I knew very little about Jewish history and even less about religion, tradition, or culture. I went to Waspy private and Catholic schools.

So, I am on my way to the Middle East. At least that's my intention when I arrive at New York's Kennedy Airport on a Sunday afternoon to board an El Al flight to Tel Aviv.

A row of low-slung wooden tables stretches across the room in front of the Israeli airline's ticket counters. Queues of people with their suitcases staggered alongside them extend from these benches all the way back to the doors that allow entrance to El Al's check-in area. No one flying to Tel Aviv is exempt from scrutiny.

For reasons of security, every passenger is subject to routine questioning before they're allowed to check in, but in my case, the questions and answers have skewed noticeably from the routine. Even worse, my "story" is suspect; at least that's what the young Israeli security person insinuates as she disappears with my passport and airline ticket. Minutes later she returns with a more experienced colleague, and the interrogation begins anew.

"Are you going to Israel for business or pleasure?"

I hesitate before answering, unsure myself why I have decided to go to Israel. "I'm a photojournalist and want to work there for a while," I say.

The Israeli security agent gestures at the two camera bags placed on the bench between us. "Is that your own personal equipment?" he asks.

I tell him yes, the cameras belong to me.

"Who do you work for?" he wants to know.

I explain that I freelance for various American news publications.

"May I see your press card?"

Since I'd left my New York City press badge at home, figuring it wouldn't be of any use in the Middle East, I show him a letter from *Newsday*, one of the newspapers I'll be stringing for. Addressed to Israel's Government Press Office, it requests that I be issued the appropriate foreign press credentials upon arrival. The security agent reads the letter. Then he studies my passport, discovers it's valid for travel to and from Israel and South Africa only, and wants to know why. I tell him I really don't know. The U.S. State Department issued the passport, and that's what they wrote.

"But why does it say Israel and South Africa?" He seems offended. "Do you have another passport?"

"Yes," I acknowledge.

"Why do you need two passports?"

"For the same reason all foreign journalists covering the region do. One can be used anywhere, and the other I need for going in and out of Israel." His eyes immediately harden. "Look, you know as well as I do that if your passport's been stamped by Israel you can't travel anywhere else in the Middle East. Except Egypt, that is."

"May I see your other passport?"

I hand over my second passport reluctantly. He examines it for some minutes and begins grilling me about why I've been to Libya. I tell him the truth. I went to Libya for *Time* magazine.

"Isn't five weeks an unusual amount of time to spend in a place like Libya?"

"Yes, I suppose it is."

"Who paid for your trip?"

"*Time* magazine."

"I'm not sure I understand what you were doing there."

"Me either," I joke, wondering which is worse: to be detained by the Libyans or interrogated by the Shin Bet, the Israeli security service. "Honestly, I was trying to take pictures but the fact is, I spent most of the time imprisoned in my hotel."

He doesn't smile. Again he wants to know why I'm not carrying a press card. It seems he wants further proof I'm bona fide foreign press. I notice that everyone waiting in line behind me is annoyed, and suddenly his disbelief irks me. I show him a copy of a letter from *Time* magazine that by chance I'd left in my passport folder. Addressed to Libya's Ministry of Information, the letter affirms I was on assignment there. It doesn't satisfy him.

Now he wants to know why I've been to Jordan. And isn't it odd that my visa to Jordan is valid for one year? And why do I have a six-month, multiple-entry visa to Lebanon? And what am I going to be doing in Israel? I look at my watch. He asks me why I'm nervous. I tell him I'm not nervous but exasperated. They've been questioning me for almost forty minutes. I'd like to know what the problem is. He says something in Hebrew to the young woman agent. As she walks away he comments quietly that if I really am a journalist, I'd understand their problems.

"You know," he says, "someone may ask you to carry something that doesn't belong to you. We have to be very careful."

I assume he's talking about explosives, so I add: "But if that's what you're concerned about, then why don't you open my bags?"

He says it's not necessary. The woman reappears with another interrogator, who seems to be head of security, and again I'm cross-examined. All I want to do is get on the plane, but he wants to know who paid for my airline ticket. I tell him I did.

"Isn't it peculiar that your newspaper didn't buy it for you?"

I reply no, it's not peculiar since I'm not staff. The head of security looks unconvinced, so I further explain that my expenses are paid for only when I'm on a specific assignment.

"But I thought you were working for *Newsday* . . ."

All the while I'm trying to stay calm, trying to be patient, but our perceptions of each other are getting more and more wayward. While the traveling I've done may raise their eyebrows, it's difficult to accept my integrity being questioned. What I see is an American Jewish photographer who thinks she wants to work in the Middle East, despite the potential complications and danger. But what they are looking at is an anonymous newsperson who has stamps in her passport from some of the countries most hostile to Israel. On top of that, she is young and single, and for sure they've read *The Little Drummer Girl*.

Now he asks where I'll be staying in Israel, and who is paying for that. And may he have the telephone number of my editor at *Newsday*. I don't like giving out anyone's home phone number, so I tell him I've only got the office numbers with me but it's Sunday, and no one will be in.

"Isn't it abnormal to be in the news business and not know your editor's home number?"

I give him the telephone number, thinking if I don't, I'll never be allowed on the plane. One of the security agents goes off, presumably to call my editor, leaving me fretting about what's going to happen if he's not home. Lucky for me, he's there and my "story" checks out. Yet the questions continue: have I been to Israel before; who do I know there; did I pack my bags myself; were they with me the whole time; how did I get to the airport; was it possible that someone could have slipped something into one of my suitcases without my knowing; and by the way, was I carrying any weapons?

An hour and ten minutes after the inquiry began, it abruptly concludes. The woman slaps yellow stickers onto my camera and duffel bags. At this I'm relieved. Had it been the red stickers, my suitcases would have been unpacked and every item examined, squeezed, or meticulously taken apart. Next comes a body search with clothes on. And if there are still any questions, a strip search.

I am finally allowed to check in at one of the El Al ticket counters, after which I pass through the carry-on X-ray security and then call *Newsday's* photo editor.

"What was that all about?" he asks.

"I haven't the foggiest. Security's incredibly tight, and I've been to all the wrong countries. They won't even tell us what gate the plane's boarding from."

"Christ," he says, "that bastard actually refused to believe I was *Newsday's* photo editor until I finally got mad and told him to call the managing editor."

―――――

Thirteen hours later, as my plane touches down at Ben Gurion Airport, everyone—men and women, young and old, religious and secular—begins clapping wildly. The gesture is emotional, sentimental, spontaneous. I think something has happened that I didn't see. Years later, I will realize that this delirium, to which I have been witness, was connected to a hidden subcurrent in their lives. From the very moment the wheels graze the runway, an ancient dream metamorphoses from a mystical kind of symbol into something visible before their eyes, a nation of their own. We have arrived safely in Israel.

―――――

I am standing in the stone courtyard of the American Colony Hotel in Jerusalem scanning the front page of the *Jerusalem Post*, the local Israeli English-language daily. The headlines jump out at me: "Man killed as rocket hits Arab bus in Jerusalem."

The rocket, fired at point-blank range, ripped a thirty-centimeter hole in an Arab bus en route to Bethlehem. The bus was moving slowly and crammed with Palestinian workers and shoppers returning home. If the shoulder-launched weapon had hit ten centimeters lower, there would have been ten times as many casualties. As it was, one Palestinian was killed and eleven others wounded, many of them lacerated by shrapnel.

A note left at the scene was handwritten in Hebrew. The authors of the letter, who called themselves "the avengers," stated that for every Jew killed, they would kill two Arabs because, in their opinion, the government does not deal firmly with them. The immediate motive of the attack was to avenge the murder of two Israeli students that had taken place four days earlier. In that incident, a twenty-two-year-old Palestinian man from the Dehaishe refugee camp shot an Israeli couple in their early twenties hiking in the wadi below the Cremison monastery near Beit Jalla. He tied them to a tree in the Bethlehem countryside, covered their faces with rags, and executed them with one bullet each to the head.

The Israeli newspapers are filled with articles about mayhem. Jewish terrorists are on trial, accused of planting car bombs that amputated the legs of two West Bank Palestinian mayors; of conspiring to blow up the Dome of the Rock, the most sacred mosque in Jerusalem; and of planting powerful bombs beneath the chassis of five Arab-owned buses, which fortunately were detonated minutes before they were timed to explode. The more I read, the more it's difficult to distinguish between what the paper calls Arab terrorism and Jewish counterterrorism.

After unpacking, I lie down on my bed, fall asleep, and dream. The scene takes place in one of those great old Arab courtyards with a mosaic inlay crisscrossing its stone floor and a vine tree overhead, oozing oversize green grapes. Off to the side, a gigantic cheesecake sits on a round marble-topped table. The courtyard swarms with Arabs and Jews, except instead of shaking hands they swap faces, so that everyone is getting confused about who is who. In the meantime, the host is slicing cheesecake faster and faster, trying to fill the demand, which is more and more pressing. Miraculously, the cake continues delivering, although he's doled out more than could possibly exist. What is this supposed to mean, I wonder after I awake. The burning bush that is not consumed? Palestine? The proverbial cake that everyone wants a piece of?

————

The following day, in opening a debate on terror in the Israeli Knesset, Police Minister Haim Bar-Lev states: "The basic question we must ask ourselves with respect to Arab and Jewish terror is whether we believe in a single standard of morality or a double standard—one for Jews and one for Arabs. Counter-terror only incites further terror; it is the height of irresponsibility."

How much more than an arbitrary border stands between these men called enemies?

2

Reorienting

(OCTOBER 1984)

I walk through the massive archway at Damascus Gate feeling small and overwhelmed by the seductive power of this city. The immediate present is compelling in the noisy, dissonant market. From under her roof, the Old City bustles with merchants' cries that entice, urge, and plead with me to buy, eat, stop for coffee, come see. People thrust forward, shoes scuffing stone, jostling to overtake each other in the narrow corridors. A child rushing off on a beat-up bike collides with two tourists. Falafel sizzles in hot oil. The muffled voices of young men dawdling wafts through the air like the smoke of their cigarettes. A trio of holy men darts around a corner. A donkey clip-clops lazily down the alleyway. Lamentations echo in the distance like a mysterious prediction. Jerusalem ticks, and from the eyes of an outsider this stubborn vitality is unforgettable.

I listen to the cadence of the languages, trying my best to absorb the sounds, to distinguish their shape. They are as old as the seasons and as different in texture as summer and winter. Hebrew is unconstrained. It sallies forth like an ocean storm, causing turbulence and commotion. Unabashedly frank and straightforward. Nothing's hidden, nothing concealed. Arabic is self-possessed. It unfolds as the desert, all swirls and aesthetics. A language of manners, it cajoles and alludes. One must sort through the layers to discern its illusions.

I crisscross the city with its myriad faces—Russians, Germans, Austrians, Yugoslavs, French, Swedes, Iraqis, Moroccans, Yemeni, Americans, Canadians, Brazilians, and Argentineans. They all look the same: resilient, determined, frustrated, unsmiling. What brings them here? A need to know the stories behind the faces and the incidents consumes me.

At twilight the walls of ancient Jerusalem ascend from the burial grounds of bygone civilizations, challenging omniscience. The past breathes in the smooth-layered face of her stone, invoking images of those courted by Jerusalem's legend. Men have fought over her since the reign of David and before, taking hold of her body with a conqueror's arrogance, laying claim to her limbs, as if conquest thus forced endures. But this is the fallacy of the occupier's imagination. Mortal competitors lie beneath Jerusalem's bones, their memory preserved in the remains of endless conflict, endless carnage. Jerusalem towers heavenward through the silvery-gray of dusk's decline, destiny's holy mourner.

I will befriend the stones, for in their age lies the wisdom of posterity. I will learn from this land, for in its roots dwell the history of men's battles. I will submit to the strangeness, relying on the sun for warmth and the moon for nourishment.

_____

I get into the habit of going each morning to one of the sidewalk cafes, where I have a cup of cappuccino and a croissant, read the paper, and watch the steady flow of people. It's not far from Beit Agron, the government-run press building, where later I go to check out press releases. Breakfast is terrible and served with the usual Israeli insolence. I am not impressed with the manners of the young Jewish population. They communicate at the top of their lungs only. They never smile.

I discover La Belle's, a restaurant/bar and hangout for both local and foreign journalists. In the daytime, foreign journalists walk across from Beit Agron for lunch and a few drinks before filing their stories. In the evenings it's a local haunt. For the most part, the local and foreign press don't mix. The foreign press is here to cover the story, not to intermingle in the culture. I want to do both.

I sit at a table by myself. Over time, a few heads nod in my direction. News mongrels are a breed in themselves. They can be a tough, macho coterie. When you relocate, even if you're already professionally established, it takes time before you're accepted into the tribe, especially for a woman. Yet I like being here, listening to the exaggerated accounts of real-life stories, drunk on war-zone adventures, as tales are swapped and legends reinvented.

"Planning to stay?" an Israeli cameraman asks me one day.

"I don't know, really. It depends. Why do you ask?"

"It's always interesting to see how long you guys last."

Eventually I'll go through enough variations on this conversation to know that "you guys" means me, the foreigner. And that we are undeserving of even the smallest courtesies because we don't pay the price of being here. The real price, that takes into account the sweat and discomfort, the tears and nightmares, the cumulative years of obligatory army and reserve duty, and the taxes that take away half an income. Me, the Jewish outsider, with the childish bleeding-heart liberalism, who comes here to examine "the story," crying out loud "but how could we," which everyone knows really means *they*; and me, the superficial, spoiled American who can walk away from it all, and who undoubtedly will, as soon as I'm bored, or tired, or fed up.

———

It grows increasingly unclear to me why people call this a "Westernized" country. The phones don't work, the press is censored, there are guns everywhere. I am perpetually uneasy. How, I wonder, can anyone relax when wherever you look, there is someone toting or pointing a machine gun? They casually rest across shoulders, carried by anybody who wants to. Will I get used to the sight of civilians wearing sandals, shorts, T-shirts, and Uzis, in movie theaters, at the supermarket, at shopping malls, and at bars? They aren't frightening as much as disconcerting.

This is a difficult country to get accustomed to. There are bomb shelters in homes and children's playgrounds, security at every store, the ever-present notion of "security reasons," the way people dress, as if they don't give two hoots about appearance (they don't). Restaurants and movies open on Fridays are stoned by the ultra-Orthodox Haredim.

Then there is the noise: Israelis always screaming, shoving, and arguing. Sometimes at night the sonic boom of fighter jets, a bevy of sirens, or an abnormally loud explosion wakes me from sleep. I wonder if something's happened and whether I should get dressed, grab my cameras, and chase the noise through the streets.

Pedestrians here smack of arrogance. When I drive, they dare me to hit them. Both Arabs and Jews. They cross the road as if in an act of defiance, their heads twisted deliberately toward me, accusation in their stony eyes: "Here I am. And even if you run me over, you cannot remove me. My body will claim this soil through the grave."

There is constant talk of survival. A land to be shared, a country to be shattered. In the newspapers, on the streets. Everyone is obsessed. An Arab is shot, a Jew is stabbed. The appropriate demonstrations ensue. Palestinian youth, their rebellious features masked in black-and-white keffiyehs, flaunt PLO flags and throw stones at Israeli vehicles. Indignant Jewish settlers assault sleeping Arab villages, shattering windows and slashing tires. The Israeli army sprays tear gas and rubber bullets. Towns are put under curfew. The wounded are taken to hospitals. Arrests are made. This is the news.

I have no understanding of this place, nothing to fit it into. I am confused and disoriented, trying to feel my way. Nothing here is easy. It is a place where you wake up and never know what will happen. A place of emotions, of spirit, of passion, of madness, and an awesome beauty, engulfed by a past too old to recognize, yet too familiar to lay quiet within me. Why does this land make me quiver?

Beneath all the smells, the images, and the noise, there is a silence, the type of silence that brings everything to a standstill. A stubborn silence. A silence of struggle, of tension, of questions that remain unanswered. How long will we be here (Israelis); and how long can we remain like this (Palestinians)? It is this silence I want to photograph.

———

Rabbi Moshe Levinger stands by the side of the road, as he has for days, as he will for three months. Like a mule, he's got something in his head, and there's no reasoning with him. Opposite him sits the Deheisha refugee camp, a hotbed of rebellious discontent. Between them lies the main thoroughfare through Jerusalem, Bethlehem, and Hebron. Two army jeeps are parked nearby with a dozen or so soldiers in close proximity.

Levinger is the spiritual leader of the Gush Emunim settler's movement in Hebron. He says he'll camp outside Deheisha until Palestinians quit pelting Israeli cars with stones. I watch the soldiers guarding Levinger while he stares silently at Deheisha. Some of the residents have gathered, their arms folded across their chests as they gaze back at him.

Two carloads of demonstrators from Israel's Peace Now movement arrive. They line themselves up in front of the camp, holding big cardboard placards that say "Stop the terror of the settlers against Deheisha," and "Disarm the phalangists of Gush Emunim!"

A very old, frail Arab man walks across the road, cradling an infant in his arms. He holds the child out toward Levinger as a plea for recognition. But the rabbi shuts his eyes, genuflecting as he mutters his morning prayers.

A bus pulls into the scene, dropping off a crowd of Israeli teenagers. They huddle around Levinger, chanting: "We will never give it up, Judea and Samaria. Never!" The soldiers are relaxed beside their jeeps, apparently under orders to not interfere.

The same Arab reappears carrying a silver tray of steaming mint tea, which he now offers with the gracious manners of a servant to the Peace Now demonstrators.

In a few weeks' time, the rabbi will abandon his vigil but not his reactionary efforts. Armed settlers will storm the camp in the middle of the night, shooting at homes and throwing rocks through windows. The next day, the army will enclose the camp with eighteen-foot-high wire mesh "to stop the stones," they say. Afterward young children can be seen pressing their noses to the fence.

Rabbi Levinger will win his battle against Deheisha.

————

In Hebron, a Jewish settler patrols one of the narrow side streets behind the Arab souk. He is burly with a dark, tangled, overgrown beard. An Uzi is slung across his back, its barrel pointed down at the sidewalk within quick reach of his right arm. He is flanked by a German shepherd. A Palestinian man advances toward them on a donkey. As the donkey draws near, the dog lets out a deep-throated growl and instinctively lunges at the other animal. The shepherd is pulled back mid-leap and rewarded with a biscuit. The donkey ambles on. A few minutes later a Palestinian boy of six or seven, lean and a bit scruffy, wants to pass but hesitates when he sees the dog. The settler taunts the boy for his timidity. As the embarrassed boy goes to move, the shepherd snarls. Laughing, the settler restrains his pet and pats its head. The boy races past.

————

I learn to recognize Palestinians by their age. The young children are sad and sweet, with too much knowledge in their faces. They have seen too much. Adolescence is a mask, watchful and unsure. The young men are rebellious and suspicious. Eventually, emotions harden behind a mask again, impenetrable. Women wear faces of strength and resilience. Old men, their expressions lost, are stripped of pride and dignity. They are passive, their eyes almost glazed.

————

In the Jordan Valley, an area of farmland has just been possessed by the Israeli army. Palestinian families sit huddled together with their belongings — pots, pans, armchairs, tattered clothing, whatever they could gather quickly enough. Pickup trucks are being loaded. Their homes have been demolished by bulldozers and the harvested land plowed over. They have been told to go elsewhere. It looks like there was a tornado here.

I shoot quickly, afraid the army will return and tell me to leave. I'm stopped instead by one of the Arabs, an elderly farmer. "Can I ask you a question?" he says. "It's your dollars that support this. Can you tell me why you are doing it? What does America have against us?"

I don't know how to answer him, so I tell him I'm sorry, that's why I'm photographing.

"You should take the picture from the sky," he says softly, "not from the land. Only then can you really show what's happened here."

I return to the same spot the next day. The land is empty, everyone has gone. Then I see a solitary old woman carrying a pail. From the distance I photograph her as she sinks to the ground, looks up to the sky, and then with swollen hands gathers some earth from the place she once lived until her green bucket is filled to the brim. With one hand still in the ground she pushes herself up from her knees. She pats the deep dark grains of soil. With her bucket full of memory, she slowly walks to wherever elsewhere might be, not once looking back.

———

It begins to rain. Low, dirty-gray clouds hang overhead. They seem to be crying; tears streak the landscape, fall onto the camera around my neck, clinging to the hood that protects the lens. A sallow, turbid gloom filters through the valley, settling along the hillside's slopes, reducing visibility. I slip on the rocky terrain, cursing the sullen weather, the weight of my camera bag, a hole in my right sneaker, and Israelis. So far the day has been miserable.

In the last forty-eight hours, two Palestinian students have been killed by the Israeli army during demonstrations. I rush off to the small West Bank village of Nebi Sallah to photograph one of the funerals, but the group of soldiers there has other thoughts. An army jeep is parked across the narrow road sideways, obstructing the road into the village. A TV crew argues with the soldier in charge, but he is adamant. "We don't want any trouble; the area is closed to the press." The crew storms off, the wheels of their car screeching.

I drive on to the University of Bir Zeit where, according to the TV crew, a demonstration will be taking place. Soldiers block all entrances to the West Bank campus. "You'll have to leave," they say. "No press allowed." Now I am really vexed. It seems the only way around the army today is to leave the car behind and hoof it through the olive groves.

I trudge determinedly along the steep goat path that someone said leads to Bir Zeit, picking my way between the stones, walking endlessly on and on through the drizzle into the desolate middle of nowhere, feeling more and more like an idiot. Three kilometers and a sloshing sneaker full of mud later, from the brow of the hillside I suddenly see hundreds of students assembling. An enormous white banner is unfurled, bearing the inevitable slogans denouncing Israel in blood-red Arabic lettering. Posters of Yasser Arafat are thrust in the air, and the forbidden PLO flag is raised.

I shoot half a roll as the demonstration begins, leaving the day's frustration behind. The light's smoky tone lends mood to the image. Then, scrambling down the hill, I'm propelled into motion by the marching, chanting crowd. I shoot swiftly, snatching the image of pictures that pull me into their orb. The rhythmic crush moves student faces in and out of focus, and once again I'm drawn into my world through theirs.

The demonstration disperses peacefully, and someone offers to give me a lift. "Why is it," he says on the way, "that everyone thinks Palestinians have nothing to give? I can't teach my son to think about killing and war all the time. I want him to breathe the air freely."

He drops me off at my car. I head south toward Jerusalem, then compulsively veer right, driving into Ramallah, where yesterday's shooting incident occurred.

The town is under curfew. The shops are closed, their aluminum doors tightly locked. The Arabs themselves have gone, vanished to who knows where, as if they never existed. For half an hour I frame wide-angle shots of the eerily empty streets. A soldier walks down a street alone, the expression on his face unforgettable. He looks back over his left shoulder, alarm in his deep-set young eyes. Despite his macho stride and sophisticated ammunition, he is vulnerable. He doesn't see any Palestinians, but he's afraid for his life. Afraid of the unpredictable. It's part of his manner. He can't help it. The silence is unnerving.

———

Moussa is a soft-spoken, medium-aged Palestinian with startling green eyes. He owns a popular late-night kosher restaurant in a Jewish quarter of Jerusalem. He tells me he has many Jewish friends, literally some of his best friends. He lives in a village called Surif, just north of Hebron, and excepting Fridays (the Muslim day off), Moussa commutes back and forth daily. Like many West Bank towns, Surif has a history. In 1948 a group of thirty-five Jewish soldiers was slaughtered as they walked through the village on their way to a settlement. A few days after Israel's Six-Day War, the village was assaulted in retaliation.

Moussa's decided to give a feast at his home. About twelve of us are invited. I've offered to drive my Israeli neighbor Yehuda plus three other guests. We pull up in front of Moussa's house the day of the party, and I wait until everyone's out of the car to lock up. Yehuda tells me not to. I think about it and realize he's right. Moussa and his family are outside to greet us. We're ushered into his home and offered coffee or tea. In a short while, another car full of Israelis joins us. We're clustered around the living room, telling funny stories, big plates full of food on our laps, when I notice one of the guests has a pistol stuck in the back of his belt. I look around the room carefully and spot another Israeli gun, not quite as obvious. I wonder if Moussa and his family have seen the guns and how they must feel if they have. Then something about the car worries me. I don't know why.

I excuse myself for a minute. In the car, there are more weapons, under the passenger's seat where Yehuda sat. We've come to Moussa's home as a friendly battalion, ready to accept his hospitality—even more ready should the friendship turn sour.

———

"Dixie" is a code name for Israel, hatched some years ago, though I don't know exactly when, by someone among the foreign press corps. I can imagine a swarm of restless journalists clustered around Beirut's Commodore Hotel bar, deciding quite suddenly to earmark a password for the land that in many an Arab capital must not be mentioned by name. An ordinary afternoon during which the legendary choice of a euphemism was contrived, decreed and, ever since, handed over like a press card to new hacks traveling the region.

———

The land is so beautiful. The Jordan Valley: fertile, productive, time-worn. In the middle flows the Jordan River—a skinny stream of biblical water that pious Christians submerge themselves in. It has also become a border, separating the Hashemite Kingdom of Jordan from the Israeli-occupied West Bank. A parade of flagpoles is planted firmly into the earth, a semi-arc around the soft bend of the foothill in front of me. The blue Star of David flaps with audacity. I follow the flags' path, counting fourteen of them. There is no one in sight, and the flags seem to lead to nothing in particular. Their only purpose appears to be to stake this stretch of West Bank territory. I want to capture this image, but it's midday and the harsh desert light will ruin the picture. I return the next day very early in the morning, but the flags are gone. For three days I search, driving and driving, thinking maybe I mistook the place. The vision has disappeared as abruptly as it came. Perhaps it was a mirage. Or an omen. Or a premonition of things to come.

———

"Why are you here? You're not Israeli."
"The last one like you lasted six weeks."
"We'll see to it that you don't work."
"There's nothing here for you. Move to Denmark. Move to Jordan. Maybe you'll find something there."
"Why would you live here? You have an American passport."
"I'm staying," I say.

3

Crossing the Bridge

(NOVEMBER 1984)

I've been in Israel one month now. I'm thirty, an outsider, and alone. Yet I feel connected to everything—the sounds, smells, and faces, the dust and the relentless sun that drives white-hot shafts of glaring light through the shimmering heat, leaching nearly every scene I squint at.

In a hired car, a driver takes me toward the "green line," a boundary marker that separates Israel from the territories captured in 1967. There is no fence. Nor has anyone grabbed a bucket of paint and drawn a green stripe down the length of the country. Yet there are so many lines here, borders that are indistinct, thoughts and actions that crisscross, set in a kind of limbo. As we drive across Jerusalem, this invisible border sets East apart from West, isolates Arab from Jew. This too, of course, is partially an illusion. As with many other things, over time the line of demarcation has changed, the peripheries made less distinct, causing further upheaval in the history of the landscape.

We head south around the Old City. To my right, glittering high above the ancient walls, is a golden dome cast against the sky. The Dome of the Rock is where the Prophet Mohammed leaped upon his horse and rode into Heaven. The hill to my left is the Mount of Olives, where Christ ascended into Heaven. Upon its slope there is a vast Jewish graveyard, opposite the gate through which the Messiah will enter Jerusalem on the Day of Judgment. Monuments, shrines, tombs, and places of worship commemorate the spiritual impulses of centuries, the perennial need for prayer in the form of meditation, and the call for redemption, atonement, salvation, and deliverance. Prayers are spoken daily in the languages of three of the world's great religions; altruistic concerns about the preservation of humanity abound, though irreconcilable claims mitigate against peaceful coexistence.

We cross the green line, traveling now through the West Bank, although there are no road signs that tell me so. I'm off to Jordan this morning, through the territory that was lost to Israel during the Six-Day War, land that some claim to be historically part of the Jewish state while others hope it will one day be a Palestinian homeland.

From Jerusalem it takes two and a half hours to get to the northern border with Lebanon and Syria. It takes one hour to get to the Mediterranean coast, three hours to the southern border with Egypt, and forty-five minutes to the Jordan River. One cannot drive more than a couple of hours in any direction without encountering a hostile border and having to turn around. This is one way to understand Israel's isolation, its sense of insecurity.

The Arab town of Bethany blends into the landscape. Terraces of olive trees, planted centuries ago, wind through the town. The stone houses are welcoming, with soft archways that open onto guest porches in the classic style of Palestinian architecture. It is a place of pilgrimage, for Lazarus rose from the dead here. Along the road, a sprinkling of one-room cafes proffer tea to any traveler who stops. There is an air of timelessness. A village life of farmers intimate with the soil, who rely on the slow changing of seasons, their hands understanding the age of the earth.

Later I will discover just how wrong this impression is. A younger generation inevitably bears the discontent of a life muddled by political limbo. They will bring new ideas into the village, and they will demand a new reality they can call their own.

Further down the road, the Jewish settlement of Ma'aleh Adumim took a chunk of land belonging to the people of Bethany. Built circularly on a mountaintop, the settlement exudes its own persona, its architecture haughty yet introverted, like a fortress in a moat of fear. Steep slopes, empty of any dwellings, cut the settlement off from the rest of the landscape, insulating insider from outsider. The settlers have created a world for themselves alone, as if physical separation can erase the effects of unlawful possession of land.

Their siege mentality is buttressed by language itself, a geographic war of words in which verbal sovereignty over the land is fought for. The settlers insist that the West Bank be called the Old Testament names for these regions, Judea and Samaria. Throughout the West Bank, Arabic names for cities and towns have been dislodged or removed from existing maps and road signs and changed to biblical or Hebrew names.

We drive past a small Bedouin encampment with dark brown tents, some children, and a flock of sheep bunched together. A few minutes later, there is nothing to look at but the vast emptiness of the Judean hills.

There is nothing but the landscape itself, only the solitude of its sorrel-colored slopes and wide, voluptuous curves undulating in front of me. On this stretch of the highway, my sense of being an outsider collapses, the feeling of being a foreigner disintegrates. There is something about this sweep of sand and stone mountain, with its raw primeval beauty, to which I belong. I don't need to claim it as the settlers have, but I feel anchored and at home.

Or perhaps the land is at home in me. Given my sentiments toward those Jews who have settled across the green line, this feeling is more than a little unsettling. I have seen other landscapes that are objectively more magnificent. Yet I still find this to be the most beautiful and gripping place on earth, though I know so little about my own roots. My family immigrated to America from Russia, France, Germany, and elsewhere, but the history and the original family names have all been lost, forgotten, or erased from memory during the periods of assimilation. So much is buried. There are no stories or even secrets to fantasize about.

The hills descend quickly toward the Dead Sea, whose faded blue contours circumscribe the lowest point on earth. The car turns west, slowing down to weave through the first Israeli checkpoint on the road that leads to Jericho. Lush plots of green vegetation seem out of place in the dry, pristine whiteness of the Jordan Valley. Farms, watered carefully against the heat, glisten with rebirth. On the opposite side of the road sprawl the abandoned mud-brick remains of a refugee camp called Aqabat Jabar. The homes are in ruins, crumbling back into the earth, becoming part of the desert again. I walk through the camp and feel disturbed by the feeling of exile, of time and place lost in the lives of those who have vanished. There is something about it I want to frame.

The Aqabat Jabar refugee camp, I've been told, is nicknamed "twice in a generation." Palestinians fled here from their homes inside the new state of Israel when the War of Independence broke out, and then fled once again, across the valley into neighboring Jordan, during the war in 1967. Everywhere there are reminders of the past, a human silence made loud by broken walls, fallen roofs, and emptiness. Life has disappeared from the camp, leaving in its place an eerie memory of before and after.

Jericho is a warm and somnolent town. Streets are lined with palm trees, flowering bougainvillea, and shops selling sumptuous heaps of fruit picked from orchards in this oasis valley. Gardens hide behind walls of abandoned monasteries and gracious winter villas of wealthy West Bankers. Layers of dust mingle with the scent of jasmine. A bus of tourists rolls by, steering toward a great mound of excavated earth where the ruins of the world's most ancient city lie. My driver turns in the opposite direction, passing groves of baby bananas and blossoms I don't recognize but which burst here and there into red and orange splashes.

The private taxi is a roomy eight-passenger Mercedes that would normally be shared. But so little is normal here that I've hired the entire car for reasons that will soon be obvious. At the next Israeli checkpoint, a long line of Mercedes-Benzes are pulled over to the side of the road, waiting. They are filled with Palestinians. Their engines are turned off, and the trunks are open so their contents can be checked. My driver zips to the front of the line, allowed to do so because I'm a Westerner with a foreign passport. A soldier waves the car forward. All of us are heading for the Allenby Bridge, the only place from which a tourist can cross the river and enter Jordan.

Beyond the checkpoint lies a restricted military zone enclosed by a high-voltage electrified security fence. The road winds downward, descending through an area that has been swept into a sculptured series of sand canyons and desert dunes. The most strategic hills are topped by metal sentry boxes with high antennas. Soldiers survey both sides of the Jordan River, which now separates Israeli-held territory from the Arab world a mile away. You think you are on the moon until, as if out of nowhere, a small building appears with a blue-and-white Israeli flag hoisted from a nearby pole.

As my taxi shifts to a halt at the terminal, my mind automatically switches gear. I take my belongings out of the car, thinking about the strange rituals to come. Inside the waiting room, a group of Israeli soldiers drink coffee among themselves, their demeanor relaxed yet distant. Neither they nor anybody else tell travelers the procedures for crossing over the bridge to Jordan. I've arrived early to avoid the worst of the hassle. I don't want to get stuck in line, waiting to get my passport stamped. More often than not, the unwary get turned back because they have failed to pay the requisite exit tax. Re-cycled through the passport control line, they are surprised to find themselves standing at attention to stave off nervousness while their names are cleared by a computer that seems to have information on anyone who's ever passed through Israel. If the computer is down, a soldier then pulls out a massive brown ledger, searching endlessly for the appropriate identity.

When my name's been cleared, the passport official hands me a pink slip, which indicates that my documents are in order, and I can leave the territory controlled by Israel. With few exceptions, private cars and taxis are not allowed over the bridge, and it's illegal to walk, so I cannot proceed without the minibus. The problem is that the bus runs at random. An hour later, I climb aboard only to find the trip delayed by the ignorance of a handsome Austrian who wants to pay the Jordanian bus driver in

Israeli shekels. The transport service across the bridge is run by a company from Jordan under special agreement with Israel. The bus driver, who only speaks Arabic, comes from a country that officially has no relations with the Jewish state. The embarrassed traveler is forced to return to the passenger terminal and seek out the moneychanger, who will hopefully change the rest of his shekels into dinar, the currency of Jordan.

The bus finally sets out, passing another building on its way, the one through which Arabs are ushered. For the inhabitants of the West Bank and the Gaza Strip, the "open-bridge" policy makes it possible to get away from the strictures of life under occupation and rejoin the Arab world for a while, in order to study or do business, or visit family and friends.

Ironically though, in the eyes of Palestinians, the bridge has come to symbolize their ultimate lack of freedom. Israel has the power to close the bridge, in general and to specific Palestinians; to grant or deny Arabs the individual permits required for crossing; and to enact arbitrary laws that control livelihoods and lives in order to monitor comings and goings. One such decree, for instance, is that West Bankers between the ages of twenty and thirty cannot return home until at least nine months have elapsed since their departure. Any person, young or old, who has left the West Bank for a period that exceeds three years, no matter what the reason, automatically loses his natural right to return as a West Bank resident. Instead, that person must apply for a "family reunification" permit.

When all is said and done, some 400,000 people cross the bridge every year. But worst of all is the way those Palestinians returning home, or their relatives who are coming to the West Bank or Gaza for a visit, are treated. As soon as they get off the bus from Jordan, they're told to sit down on one of the plastic seats in the terminal and not move until their name is called over a loudspeaker. When that happens, they must stand in front of a counter answering questions while a soldier empties suitcases piece by piece, examining every part of every single item. Anything electrical is confiscated, as are cameras, videocassettes, film, most cosmetics, and anything else that might contain explosives or could be deemed a security threat. Toys are taken away, without exception, from tearful children, forbidden because sometimes they have been used to conceal detonators. Afterward, personal belongings are dumped into a plastic container, which, along with suitcases, gets sent to be X-rayed. The traveler goes to another hall to wait. Sometime later they're called into a small room where shoes are tossed into a crate, which, once it is full, is also taken for X-rays. Then they are made to strip down to underwear so that a soldier can, as one Palestinian put it, "check the ass of every human being." For the final humiliation, the crate of footwear is thrown back into a room, where they must scramble to spot their shoes among dozens of other pairs.

Further on are the big red trucks used by Palestinians to transport watermelon, slabs of marble, crates of vegetables, and other merchandise to Jordan. They are outlandish and, in any other country, would not be permitted on the road. Their hoods have been cut away from the engines, and their hubcaps removed. Seats have no upholstery, dashboards no gauges. Transmissions are stripped bare. Gas tanks have a transparent window so their contents can be easily seen. Any parts that could possibly hide the makings of a bomb, or an illegal weapon, have been drilled with holes, or taken off and made visible to the eye. Still the smuggling of arms, or at least the attempt, continues.

The bus pulls up in front of the last Israeli checkpoint, where a soldier steps briefly aboard to check passport pictures. A few feet beyond is the bridge itself, a dumpy wood and metal structure painted an awful kelly green. At the far end is the Jordanian position marked by a mound of tattered sandbags. Every morning, a Jordanian policeman in a blue uniform and blue beret and an Israeli soldier in green meet at the halfway point on the bridge in order to arrange certain technical details. Neither can walk past the center plank. Though they can't visit each other's country, every day a bundle of newspapers is exchanged, politics organizing the conduct between enemies, defining relations between human beings.

The thick wooden planks clatter and groan as the bus rolls onward. Beneath us flows the Jordan, brown and sluggish, edging around the relics of a part of the bridge that collapsed during the Six-Day War. Midway across the bridge I switch passports, carefully tucking the one I use in Israel into a special pocket in my camera bag. I don't want to make any stupid mistakes. Moments later the bus halts and Abu Riyad, an extremely amiable policeman with a fine sense of humor, climbs aboard and welcomes us to Jordan. He then looks through everyone's passports to make sure they have a Jordanian visa. When it is my turn, he pretends to scrutinize every single page, holding my passport in such a way that an attached leaf flutters down toward the aisle like a streamer. A smile crosses his face. "No Israeli stamps?" he says. "Are you sure?" Had he found one in my passport, I would be barred from Jordan. Though Abu Riyad knows exactly where I've come from, the myth that everyone adheres to is that I've materialized from Somewhere Else.

4

Ode to Abu Ammar

(NOVEMBER 1984)

I stand in a corner of a sports complex in Amman where television crews and camerapeople are cordoned off, witnessing the seventeenth session of the Palestine National Council, a parliament-in-exile that decides the policies of the Palestine Liberation Organization (PLO). Looking out through my lens, I spot some of the Middle East's most obstinate and legendary guerrillas.

There on the dais, wearing a light brown corduroy suit, is Khalil al-Wazir, one of the founding members of Fatah, the largest faction in the PLO. He is more widely known by his nom de guerre, Abu Jihad, which means "father of the holy war," a metaphor for his position as military commander of the PLO and architect of Fatah's "armed struggle" against Israel. He's deployed dozens of PLO commando units armed with Soviet-made AK-47s and homemade explosives. In one such murderous raid in 1978, a team of eleven fighters led by a woman infiltrated Israel by sea and hijacked a bus with sixty-three passengers on the coastal highway to Tel Aviv. A vicious shootout with the Israeli Army followed. When it ended, thirty-three Israelis and nine guerrillas were dead and eighty-two others wounded.

I focus my telephoto lens on someone walking off the stage and am startled to see Salah Khalaf, a man who rarely allows himself to be seen in public. Also known as Abu Iyad, he is head of Fatah's security and intelligence and was chief of the PLO's notorious Black September Organization until it was disbanded in 1974. He personally authorized the terrorist operation at the 1972 Olympic Village in Munich that resulted in the massacre of eleven Israeli athletes. He also supervised the 1973 execution of the new American ambassador to Sudan and the departing U.S. chargé d'affaires, who were taken hostage by eight Palestinian commandos in Khartoum and, two hours later, along with the Belgium chargé d'affaires, machine-gunned to death.

I look around the tiered auditorium, eager to locate Yasser Arafat, chairman of the PLO and leader of Fatah. The hall is filled to capacity, and to my surprise nearly all the PLO representatives are dressed like businessmen, in tailored European suits and ties. So it's easy to spot the black-and-white checkered keffiyeh that frames Arafat's unmistakably strange and familiar face. He is not on the stage but in the audience, listening intently to Abu Jihad's speech, leaping up whenever he disagrees with his deputy, frantically waving his arm to command Abu Jihad's attention. Silencing his closest confidant and colleague, Arafat argues his point passionately, microphone in hand.

Toward the end of the second day, the PLO chief is criticized for his autocratic leadership, chaotic way of operating, and tradition of secrecy. Suddenly the chairman jumps up from his front-row seat and announces with great humility that he'll be resigning. In a tone quivering with restraint, so that the boisterous hall becomes stilled, Arafat urges the council's members "to change this donkey." Before the meeting concludes, to his colleagues' astonishment, he lays his resignation on the speaker's table.

When the session resumes the next day, the deputy speaker of the Palestine National Council, Selim Zaanoun, sets aside official PLO business and proceeds to try to talk to Arafat, who's moved to the third row, out of resigning. "You belong to the Palestinian people," Zaanoun shouts emotionally, and simultaneously a whirlwind of male arms plucks Arafat from the crowd, lifts him into the air, and carries him shoulder-high to the podium.

He stands before his brethren, barely five feet tall, clutching his resignation in his hand. "You are the ones who can decide. You can say Abu Ammar go, or Abu Ammar stay," he thunders, referring to himself by his nom de guerre, "Father Builder." With the mastery of a puppeteer, he unifies even his adversaries until a chorus of middle-aged voices chants the words: "Abu Ammar stay, Abu Ammar stay."

At times, he seems to be an actor who carts his theater with him, constantly recreating his role as the embodiment of Palestinian tragedy. And in fact, Arafat's histrionics, broadcast live to the region for the first time, prove so popular that nearly 2 million Palestinians living in refugee camps in Jordan, Syria, Lebanon, the West Bank, and the Gaza Strip position themselves in front of their television sets throughout the three-day conference—which is exactly what the chairman wants as he stages his stirring reelection.

"I am a soldier of the revolution," Arafat states solemnly. "I am the last to disobey orders." And before he can sit down again, a bouquet of flowers carried by a child is thrust into his hands. He is still godfather.

A few days later, commotion suddenly swells in the lobby of Jordan's InterContinental Hotel, the headquarters for the international press corps when they visit Amman. I see a flurry of reporters circling with mikes, TV cameras, pens and pads, and photographers' strobes flashing. At the center of this squall, Yasser Arafat has alighted like an exotic butterfly. He flutters, darts, and cavorts between us all. Physically small, he's almost obscured by the contingent of bodyguards orbiting him as everyone makes their way through the lobby to the elevator, to the eighth floor, where a press conference is spontaneously convened in Room 811.

I grab a spot in the first row, amid a line crammed with kneeling photographers. Behind me are the television cameras, and behind them, the reporters. Minutes later, the head of the Palestinian movement seats himself directly in front of me, no more than seven or eight feet away.

I switch my lens to frame his features only. Up close, the face is extraordinary. Everything about it is bizarre and exaggerated, a caricature of its own cartoon. The beard meticulously trimmed to a three-day soldier's stubble. Large, fleshy, crimson lips. A dramatic nose. ("How is it that Arafat is still alive?" I will ask his advisors years later. They grin and inevitably say, "It is his nose. He can smell danger.") But it's the eyes that are his strangest feature: like large white magnets. They draw me in; I am riveted.

I can see that he is fussy about the way he dresses, to the point of being prissy. His black-and-white checkered keffiyeh is spotless, each pleat folded neatly across his head just so, and its length draped carefully along his right shoulder. Another keffiyeh is wrapped around his neck like a cravat. His olive-drab fatigues are pressed perfectly, and the handle of his revolver glistens, as does the lizard holster that is strapped to the side of his belt. His brown leisure-style boots, raised by two-inch block heels, have been polished to a luster. He has small hands, manicured nails, and no rings or jewelry, except for a Rolex on his left wrist. When a reporter once asked why he ran around in such a curious getup, he replied: "I like to dress the Arafat way!"

I snap on a wider lens to capture his gestures. Even while sitting, Arafat is in motion: wriggling a little to the left, then to the right, leaning back, thrusting forward; hands fidgeting; shaking his right forefinger at the press corps; both arms conducting when his temper flares. And all the while his feet tap to an off-sync rhythm. He is a kaleidoscope of shifting shapes, as if his life depends on it. Every time he moves I have to refocus.

Deftly, he avoids explanations, dodges new questions, contemplates how each word might be interpreted in the corridors of East and West. He speaks Arabic with an Egyptian accent and English with a fearlessness that makes his aides cringe, charming his audience with a mixture of humor and theater, playing with language until he finds a rhetorical loop at a dizzying pace.

I'm thinking about his image, the uniform that has become fixed over time, its appearance an extension of his mask, when I see his attention suddenly swerve toward me, his eyes twinkling with some kind of private amusement. Then he winks. Shamelessly. Followed by a wide toothy grin. I think to myself, "No, it can't be. I must have imagined it." He winks again. Not a flirtatious wink, but that of a man always onstage and bored. As if to say: "Come on, play. Same old boring questions; same dull answers. Who can take it seriously?" And yet it seems despair dances around the edge of his eyes.

Arafat swoops off at the end of the press conference and everyone else filters into the hotel's bar. It is my first time with the foreign press group who cover the Middle East, and everyone is there—*Time*, *Newsweek*, the big American newspapers, the British dailies, and the television networks, mostly men clustered around a long row of half-empty beers, double martinis, and scotches on the rocks. The barroom banter stimulates a play of wits among the best of commentators as they discuss the PLO's reconciliation with Hussein, the first time in fourteen years such a large-scale PLO gathering has taken place in Jordan. I walk in, the new face, edging to the side of the crowd. A few heads glance in my direction.

"So, Carol," says the one photographer I know, "what's the story with you and Arafat?"

"Yeah, let us in on the secret," says another cameraperson.

"Come on, you guys," I say. "This is the first time I've ever seen him."

"Sure! You really expect us to believe that?"

One thing is certain, whether you admire Arafat or not, his theatrics are memorable and the fact that he is still alive remarkable. He was not yet eighteen when he began smuggling arms into Palestine, and then in 1948, he fought against the birth of the State of Israel. He continued to be politically active during the early 1950s while he was a student at Cairo University, where he obtained an engineering degree—interrupting his studies to take training courses in weaponry, specializing in explosives. By the time he was thirty, he was living in Kuwait and had set up his own contracting business. It was here that the idea of an armed organization with the intention of liberating Palestinian land was first discussed with Khalil al-Wazir, Salah Khalaf, and other prosperous young exiles.

Fatah, meaning "conquest," came into existence in 1959 and is still by far the largest and most significant of a number of Palestine national liberation groups. Five years later, following a decision taken at an Arab Summit in Cairo in 1964, an umbrella movement called the Palestinian Liberation Organization was created.

There is little information about Arafat's childhood. For years he claimed to have been born in Palestine, sometimes insinuating that he was born in Jerusalem, other times stating that he was born in the Gaza Strip, although there were no known documents to back this up. It is said by some that he was a lively, uninhibited child, which is how he acquired his nickname Yasser, meaning "carefree" or "no problem." But others will tell you he was hyper-energetic, an emotional boy who liked to jump out of high windows, and who had a violent temper.

Arafat will say only that his early years were "unhappy ones." His mother died when he was four, and although he did spend some of his childhood in Jerusalem, he was raised in Egypt, where his father was a successful merchant. When a reporter eventually uncovered his birth certificate, confirming once and for all that in 1929 Mohammed Abdel-Raouf Arafat al-Qudwa al-Husseini was born in Cairo, he pleaded with her personally not to publish the secret he had deliberately concealed.

In 1967, following the Six-Day War, Arafat slipped across Israel's borders, crisscrossing the West Bank on a motorbike to recruit the local Palestinian youth, and then vanished into the landscape—an escapade of which he is immensely proud. He had already assumed the nom de guerre of Abu Ammar, before at age forty he was elected chairman of the PLO.

Then in 1974, when the Arab Summit in Rabat decided the PLO was the only legitimate representative of the Palestinian people, he was transformed into a spokesman the world could no longer ignore. A month later, he made his appearance at the United Nations, wearing an empty holster and shouting: "I have come bearing an olive branch and a freedom fighter's gun. Do not let the olive branch fall from my hands." And ever since he has been jetting from nation to nation, tirelessly waving the Palestinian flag.

Books have been written about him, documentaries aired on television. There have been interviews and articles galore. Yet it's still difficult to get a handle on his character, to identify his personal ideology or beliefs. Why should I think I could get the one true shot of him, when he has made the cover of *Time* and *Newsweek* more than any other living head of state, portrayed by the Western media as a terrorist and a freedom fighter, becoming over the years a household name?

5

Gaza Slick

(DECEMBER 1984)

I close the door behind me, stepping out into the early morning light. A chameleon slithering across the stones freezes, then changes direction, heading toward a grapevine. This house—my house—is hidden behind the walls of an alleyway in one of the oldest neighborhoods in Jerusalem. It was a find. I've rented it, and it feels good to have roots of a sort, a home base. It feels good to no longer be the new kid on the Strip.

I put my camera equipment on the backseat of my car, also a find, which I bought secondhand from a departing foreign journalist. An American television network wants to update their in-house files with some slick pictures of their new correspondent working "in the field." My day will be spent in the Gaza Strip.

Slick and Gaza are an odd couple. He's a TV-pretty correspondent dressed in a perfectly pressed, light-gray pinstriped suit to accentuate blue-gray eyes, standing in three-quarter profile toward the camera. The day is already a sweltering sauna. I wipe beads of sweat off my camera while the correspondent combs his hair.

The sun is just beginning to color Jerusalem's empty streets. I turn down the highway to Tel Aviv. Soon the landscape will shimmer, shade, and contour, disappearing into shafts of blazing white light.

I leave my car in Tel Aviv and join up with the network's television crew.

"Can you believe he's bringing them along?" the cameraman groans as we drive south toward Gaza.

"Don't forget he's new," the sound man says.

"But did you see what his wife is wearing? I mean, where do they think they're going?"

"It's the high heels that get me."

"What about the kid? How could he bring a ten-year-old child? There's got to be something wrong with him."

"I guess he doesn't read the papers. Wasn't there a Molotov cocktail thrown in Gaza's square yesterday?" I ask.

"Two. The army's still searching the area."

"Maybe he thinks we're spending the day in Haifa."

"I hate breaking these new guys in," groans the Israeli cameraman again. "How come the foreign press change their correspondents so often?"

"Because the home office thinks reporters get stale, so every three years or so, they rotate them," I say. "It's pretty much standard policy. Anyway, the journalists get tired of covering the same story after a while."

"They're lucky they don't have to live with the story."

They light cigarettes and lapse into Hebrew, talking between themselves. Unlike the multinational correspondents, the TV crews and photographers working here are almost all Israeli, or married to Israelis.

I lean my head against the backseat, half listening to a BBC radio program warning us about the need for global conservation due to the greenhouse effect. At the age of thirty, I am not a beginner to my profession nor one of its stars. I am, like countless others, good enough to make a living and experienced enough to understand the relative ease with which truth is manipulated. But what I don't know, having just moved here to Jerusalem, is how living with this story will change me and my beliefs. It will alter the way I look at photographs. It will complicate the way I see and define the relations between past, present, and future. It will slowly compel me to challenge the interpretations of events and to reexamine the presentations of reality and the meaning of images. Ultimately, it will force me to acknowledge the fleeting context in which my experience as a photojournalist is embedded. In the end, it will shatter my career.

"Do you have some identity on you?"

The cameraman's voice jolts me out of reverie. Blue and white barrels are staggered in haphazard rows across the width of the four-lane highway. A slightly raised watchtower has been built on the right, which illuminates the area at night with an array of spotlights. On the left is a cluster of dusty, green army tents. We weave around the series of barrels, stopping in front of a six-foot-long, red-and-white spiked rod. I pull out a press card and hand it through the window to a soldier. He looks us over and, with a flick of his hand, waves us through the military checkpoint.

Entering the Strip is like being plunged into Gehenna, landing with a thud in its intestines. Despite the Mediterranean lapping at its shores,

Gaza is filthy, its landscape wretched. A washed-out "Welcome to Gaza" sign hangs overhead, the municipality's feeble attempt to proffer hospitality. We turn down a series of grimy gray streets littered with the burnt remains of tires and other junkyard flammables, and overflowing garbage bins in which scrofulous cats forage. The entire Strip is only thirty miles from north to south and less than five miles wide. It shelters 700,000 Palestinians and has one of the highest population densities in the world. No matter which way we drive, I feel resentment glaring from the eyes of these people, the refugees, crammed into Gaza's unending squalor.

We swerve into a street of sand, inching around the ditches and potholes. In front of us lies a complex sight—a warren of tiny one-story shelters, patched and rebuilt over the years to become a labyrinth of alleyways, so narrow you can touch the crusty cement housing on either side. It was set up to be a temporary place for the displaced, where clusters of tents had been swiftly assembled in clearings of sand, and it is now a permanent site. The inhabitants are cast betwixt and between the vicissitudes of exile and, surrounded by well-hoed rows of cultivated earth in villages nearby, with the memory of a different kind of life, which has metamorphosed into the story of a dream, as hope in the present has faded.

The correspondent and his family pull up behind us.

"Ugh. . . . This place stinks!" the ten-year-old says. She covers her nose. "Why's it so dirty?"

"It's a refugee camp," her mother says, the heels of her shoes sinking into the sand.

"What's a refugee?"

"Someone who doesn't have a home."

"But don't they live here?"

"Well, yes . . ."

"Then why are they refugees?"

Her mother's explanation is drowned by a flock of children running toward us calling "Sura, sura" (picture). The sky is cloudless, hanging in sapphire splashes between patches of laundry slung atop an expanse of corrugated tin roofs. The air is laced with the stench of sewage oozing in rivulets down the alleys between the houses. The cameraman angles his lens to frame the correspondent's well-known features.

"This is Jabaliya," the correspondent says, "where fifty-two thousand Palestinians live."

The children clamor around us so that we can't budge without them getting in the way, ruining the picture. They pile between the correspondent and our cameras, their faces turning serious, bodies stiffening, and, as if on cue, their arms shooting high into the air, fingers shaped into the letter "V." This is not the language of American protest, a sign signifying peace. The "V" means "Victory"—a return to the homeland, "Falastin." It is an expression fusing together Palestinian history and longing.

"Bas. Yalla!" (Enough. Go away!) I shoo the kids out of range so the correspondent can be filmed with the camp sitting in the background exactly as I'd imagined. But the youngsters push even closer, leaning into our lenses. Their message echoes through years of exile, which began in 1948, when their grandparents or great-grandparents fled their homes in Palestine. It was the turning point: the first Arab-Israeli war, as the Jewish state fought for existence. Gaza Strip fell under Egyptian control while the West Bank was incorporated into the Hashemite Kingdom of Jordan. Israeli troops occupied these areas in June 1967, following their dazzling victory in the Six-Day War, which left a second wave of Palestinians displaced. Ever since, the children have been taught that, until their victory symbol becomes reality, whenever possible they must remind Israel, the Arab nations, and the world that their fate as refugees is temporary.

The correspondent turns away from the camera, distracted by the crowd gathering around his wife and child. Behind us is an empty plot of sand, flat and featureless, extending to a span of barbed wire fencing around a military outpost. The human clutter attracts some soldiers clad in army drab, shouldering tear gas canisters and M-16s. One of them asks to see our press cards. "There might be trouble," he says. "The area might be closed to the press." He tells us to wait while he radios his superior. The correspondent, agitated at the chaos, begins to argue with the soldier. In three years' time, it will be here at this very spot that the intifada erupts, as scores of youth attack the army. But this morning, the children scatter. The cameraman and I pack up our gear. We're not looking for trouble today.

———

At the Gaza Beach Elementary Girls School, the headmistress comes out to greet us when we arrive. The thin, one-story U-shaped building takes only a few minutes to tour. There is no playground or cafeteria. No library or gymnasium. No place to make music or create handicrafts or play at sports. Not even halls in which to hang drawings or hang out in between classes. Every inch of its space is partitioned into classrooms.

When the headmistress takes us into one, forty girls aged between about eight and ten look up at us, some of them smiling shyly. The walls are sooty gray and molding from dampness. There is no electricity. Sunlight spills into the classroom at diffused angles through a few small windows. I set up

my tripod at the front of the room and wait for my eyes to adjust to the dim-
ness. Lighting—be it indoors or outdoors—is the trickiest and most deceptive aspect of photography. In order to use light properly you must learn to
see rays and shadows, the potential gradations of light, and the ratios within
any given frame or visual field.

The girls sit quietly on wooden benches, three students crowded to a desk.
I study how the light falls in the room as a whole and on specific children,
from which windows. I move my tripod a few feet to the left, swivel a camera into place, and look at the creative possibilities through the perspective
of a lens. The moment the lesson begins, every child tilts forward, throwing
my computations out. When the teacher asks a question, I lose sight of their
faces behind the jumble of frantically waving hands. If a student falters over
an answer, the other girls raise their hands, shouting, "Teacher! Teacher!"
As they compete for the instructor's attention, I try to capture their eagerness
to learn and fervid desire to express themselves.

Yet there is something else, something more in their glance that has
eluded me. I change my point of view by switching to a 50 mm lens and
concentrate on a group of three. Delicate complexions. How identical they
are. Not in terms of features, but the earnest expression. And finally the
eyes. Sobriety, depth, and darkness. The lens frames an image of surface
appearances. It's up to the photographer to create meaning. For years this
classroom scene will haunt me.

For a moment the three girls gaze into my camera, and in that split second I realize what has disarmed me. I am looking into eyes that are devoid
of joy, filled with the bewilderment of a battered and threatening existence.
This is the image I want to freeze on film. This look of desire and vulnerability, pain and perplexity, the eyes of children unable to comprehend what
they have seen, struggling to make sense of the only life given them.

"Would you like to see one of the children's homes?" the headmistress
asks.

The correspondent looks at his watch.

"It's over there," she says, and points just beyond the edge of the school
to the notorious streets of Shati.

The Shati refugee camp still seethes with an inveterate rage. It is well
known for its guerrilla activities in the early 1970s, when Kalashnikov-toting
youth swarmed through its alleys. Many of the slum-like streets are sealed
with tiers of rusty barrels to curb the mobility of camp residents. Almost
everywhere red and black anti-occupation graffiti layers the outer walls of
tumbledown shanties. The correspondent looks around uneasily. Dozens
of women stand or squat in their doorways accustomed, or at least resigned,

to the gravelly taste that sticks in our throats. We walk quickly even as we film, passing through an austere landscape from which there seems to be no relief.

"Ahlan wa sahlan!" (Welcome!) The powerful arms of a matriarch sweep us behind walls into a tiny courtyard filled with the scent of jasmine and variegated displays of flowering plants. The woman wears a traditional floor-length dress of intricately embroidered coarse black cotton. A white scarf concealing her hair cascades around her shoulders, emphasizing her robust frame. Her name is Fatima. It's difficult to tell how old she is.

The house consists of two very small rooms. Fatima ushers us into one, inviting us to please sit down, and offers Arabic coffee or tea. Except for a lemon-colored cupboard containing the family's dishware, the furniture is shabby and broken-down. The plaster walls are painted royal blue, and from them hang a birdcage with a yellow parakeet in it; a transistor radio; several black-and-white family pictures, only one of which is framed; a tapestry of Jerusalem's Old City; a large poster with two snow-white, very furry kittens; and another poster, this one smaller, of a jaunty-looking lion. It is a typical refugee camp sitting room, combining the makeshift improvisations of poverty with the whimsical images of fantasy.

Fatima returns with a tray of steaming coffee, boiled with heaps of sugar and spiced with cardamom. She has handsome features, but her face is severe, unyielding, almost rigid. She leans over to refill the cameraman's glass with coffee, settles into a chair, and with candor tells us through a translator: "I have lost everything but my dignity."

We eye each other—Palestinian and Jew. She doesn't really believe the story of the 6 million Jews who perished in the Holocaust. She has not been given books to read and her mind simply can't grasp the immensity of the figures. I understand that. It is difficult for me too. But she remembers well what it was like to have her land confiscated, to be rounded up and forced to flee, to have her home taken without any compensation, and she can't forgive that even if the story is true. I understand that too. She doesn't equate the two pasts, the experiences of Palestinian and Jew. Why should she? Neither do I. Their histories are different. But she knows she is the victim of victims.

She speaks of the inescapable conflict between Arabs and Jews and the humiliations to which Palestinians are subjugated. The hundreds of military decrees that violate individual freedom, laws that even now, in this wretched camp, can take away or destroy their homes and their property. The curfews and detentions and interrogations that are employed to force Palestinians into submission but that cannot control a people's will. Her eyes waver between her guests and the space between us. A smile crosses her face as she feels her way across cultures. "One of my sons drew a picture of a Palestinian wedding, and in the picture he drew a Palestinian flag. The schoolteacher was arrested and taken to court because of my eight-year-old boy's drawing."

She finally unleashes her passion as she speaks of her children and her children's children and the unbearable uncertainty that has thrust them all to the edge. "When will you Americans realize that we too are human beings?"

"Is there a bathroom here?" the correspondent's daughter asks. She is led to a rickety door. Seconds later, "How come you don't have a toilet?"

Her mother marches over, and in a faintly strained American voice whispers to her child to hush, use whatever there is, and for God's sake, don't sit on anything—which would be difficult anyway since the toilet is nothing more than a hole in the ground.

Before we leave I glance into the other room, where a bunch of flimsy mattresses are piled against the wall for the fourteen people who live here. Yet even at night, when the mattresses are spread out on the floor, there is neither privacy nor peace. Just last week soldiers burst into the house—as they'd done several times before—shattering the family's sleep, tossing everything to the ground, terrifying the children, whose father they beat before they took away an elder brother for reasons that were never explained. And once this nightmare is experienced, it recurs again and again in the children's dreams.

———

We drive now to Rafah, a town and camp of the same name, at the southernmost tip of the Strip. By the time we arrive, a crowd, mostly women, is gathered at the coiled wire fence that stretches along the border with Egypt. When Israel withdrew from the Sinai Peninsula in April 1982, under the peace agreement negotiated in the Camp David Accords, Rafah was partitioned. Some five thousand refugees were left on the Egyptian side of the international boundary. A strip of no-man's-land and another wire fence marking the Egyptian border separate the two communities.

Almost any time of day, residents of Gaza's Rafah are huddled at the fence bellowing their family news to relatives in Egypt's Rafah. The Israeli cameraman lingers for a moment on two women dressed in billowy white headscarves and black ankle-length skirts, then pans slowly across the breadth of the border to show the television viewer a scene he has filmed dozens of times before. "And Jamil? How is his health?" a woman hollers.

"And Samira, did she have her baby? . . . Ahmed? He is a troublemaker, that one. Just like his cousin, Radwan."

The correspondent, determined to get a story, interviews several women about their fractured families. Although he's a newcomer to the region, he is also a professional who can swiftly piece together a riveting news feature. He scribbles down a few notes for his on-camera commentary, dabs his forehead with a hankie, and begins to speak.

"While the geographic division of Rafah's population is a relatively minor issue, it illustrates another searing problem for both Palestinians and Israelis. Approximately 1.4 million Palestinian refugees, many of whom live under equally deplorable conditions, are exiled in Lebanon, Jordan, and Syria. Although family reunification is permitted on a limited basis, subject to approval from the Israeli authorities, it is an exceedingly problematic and bureaucratic procedure, and nigh impossible for those refugees living in Syria and Lebanon. Even if a solution were found for West Bank and Gaza Palestinians, the plight and resentment of refugees outside these occupied territories, who not only lost their homes and their land, but have been virtually torn apart as a people, would inevitably still have to be faced."

After three takes, the correspondent wraps up his piece. Already I'm picturing the visuals from this morning that will be cut into a complex and moving prime-time television story.

We drive back through the Strip. A group of teenage boys riding their bicycles home from school are hassled by soldiers. They have been ordered off their bikes and forced to stand in a straight line while their identity cards are checked and their school bags searched. It's the kind of image that camerapeople look for, a typical "occupation-type" scene. We drive on. After several hours, we are all anxious to get out of Gaza.

6

Photo Op

(FEBRUARY 1985)

I'm standing in the huge lobby of the InterContinental Hotel in Amman once again, here for *Newsweek*. In the next day or so, there'll be a meeting between Hussein bin Talal, the king of Jordan, and Yasser Arafat, which I'm supposed to photograph. After a fifteen-year-long feud, the two leaders have patched up their differences and agreed to work together to try to find a solution to the "Palestinian problem." Arafat is due to arrive at any moment, and even the possibility of a peace process in the Middle East always makes a story.

While the international press reporters cluster around our hotel talking about the politics of peace, I'm off to the palace with the photographers and TV crews to cover the meeting between King Hussein and Arafat. Politicians are by nature opportunists and dreamers, as are photojournalists. In their role as image-makers, both have a kind of surrealistic approach to life, each intent on conveying their vision of the world, each compelled to gaze into reality and sell "truths" to an audience.

The king's home, sandstone in color, is situated on a hill not far from the center of the city. It looks more like a comfortable villa than the palatial, showy mansions belonging to most Arab royalty. We stand in front of the residence and, moments after being positioned, a silver-gray Mercedes pulls up. Arafat springs out of the car. King Hussein, a soft-spoken, strong-minded, short, yet powerfully built man, walks down the portico steps to receive him. They pause in front of our cameras for the traditional Arab greeting, a hug and a kiss on both cheeks, then walk back up the stairs and disappear inside.

We are not shooting the event itself. In fact, we are not permitted to attend the real meeting between Hussein and Arafat in which they discuss their differing views concerning a peace accord. Instead, we have been given access to a pre-scripted event in which the visual atmosphere and setting is controlled, a "photo op," meaning, quite literally, an opportunity that has been staged specifically for photographic coverage during which reporters are generally not allowed. The photographs become news illustrations that confirm something has happened. They document the event although the above scene, as an example, lasts for less than three minutes. The image of Hussein with Arafat will be reproduced in news magazines, in papers, and on television, giving importance to the meeting regardless of any real significance it might have.

Despite their public reconciliation and our photographs, the relationship between Arafat and the king is still uneasy, even bitter. For thirty-five years, King Hussein has shaped a nation, easing a tribal kingdom into modernity and political moderation. But Jordan's borders have been reshaped by war with Israel, and its citizenry altered by a flood of Palestinian refugees. Its security has been undermined by the struggles between the Jewish state and the neighboring Arab nations, and by the fury of the stateless Palestinians.

Ever since the Six-Day War, when Hussein lost the West Bank and Jerusalem to Israel, he has been in a precarious position. At least half of Jordan's population of 3 million is Palestinian, with almost 850,000 registered as refugees. By 1970, the PLO had created a state-within-a-state in Jordan, and Arafat, along with George Habash, the leader of a radical faction of the PLO called the Popular Front for the Liberation of Palestine, triggered a civil war. In September 1970, after a spectacular series of plane hijackings that further undermined the security of Jordan, Hussein ordered his army to purge his kingdom of the PLO guerrillas once and for all in what is remembered by Palestinians as "Black September."

Ten minutes later there is another photo op: Hussein and Arafat sitting on plush, pale-blue armchairs next to each other. They smile into our cameras to show the world their revived camaraderie. Click. The setting is intimate. Click. They are serious. Click. When I photograph my mind becomes blank, usually not thinking critically. I have time only to concentrate my eye, refocus my lens, and get as many frames as possible.

In a way I can now see how we have been accomplices or tools in uniting their worlds, linking them together through images, even though we know these pictures to be artificial, their point of view as deceptive as the initial embrace. There can be little doubt that photojournalists are used by political leaders, and vice versa. We exploit each other, sometimes forming odd, but symbiotic, relationships. Our fame and fortune is in their hands;

their public image is in ours. Each of us is looking for our own moments. Each can gain a kind of immortality if the images are preserved. But with this particular story only the photographs will endure, to be recycled a year later when the peace talks between the king and Arafat collapse, as they seem destined to do.

7

A Room with a View

(APRIL 1985)

Red neon floats high across a rooftop on Madison Avenue between Forty-eighth and Forty-ninth streets, the characters identifying the headquarters of *Newsweek*. This is where scores of correspondents and photographers, who routinely rove through troubled regions in order to witness some of man's maddest moments, send their reportage. In the heart of this midtown Manhattan skyscraper a professional staff of editors, writers, and researchers compiles material coming from five continents, trying to hone raw reality into the magazine's glossy format. By the end of each week, the list of stories has shrunk, the stories themselves ordered and reorganized with a few extra quotes and some opinions thrown in.

I'm in New York to see Jimmy Colton, the editor who decides which photographers should be assigned to the international stories *Newsweek* is planning each week. There are only five overseas photographers who have a contract with *Newsweek*; the rest are hired per story. Jimmy must keep abreast of what's happening across the globe and, in addition, be certain someone is at the scene to record those unexpected events that in any given week may suddenly run in pictures. From discussions we've had recently, I know he needs someone to cover the Middle East. After six months in Jerusalem, I'm in a kind of limbo. Chasing after news is an expensive and competitive affair. Having survived ten years in the business, I'm sure of work, but I still have to be paid. Photography equipment must be cared for. And the cost of living in Jerusalem is much higher than I'd expected. So when I received a call from Jimmy saying that if I'm really serious about staying in the Middle East, we should talk, I got on a plane.

A gigantic blowup of the week's cover hangs on a white wall in the foyer of the building, where a lone security guard stands watch. Only those with

Newsweek ID cards are allowed to enter the elevators that will take them into the offices above. Visitors are assigned a guest pass. While they wait for authorization, the magnified *Newsweek* cover is distracting, insisting upon the power of a single image.

My first assignment for *Newsweek* was in 1976. I had been in Haiti at the time on a photography fellowship and thought it would be interesting to cover the Jamaica elections. It was rumored that the elections would be turbulent. In truth, I had no idea at the time what "covering" something meant, particularly a news story. But I had discovered that the press generally stayed at one hotel, and I thought that if I flew to Kingston and found the hotel that the correspondents had checked into, I could wing it from there. Fortunately, I ran into the *Newsweek* correspondent—a man I'd met previously in Haiti. By chance, *Newsweek* didn't have a photographer there, and the story was smoldering, so he was kind enough to suggest to New York that I be put on assignment. My first news photograph was published, and from then on, I had an open door to the publication.

The picture department itself, known as "Photo," occupies the entire third floor of the building. At any one time, a handful of the several dozen photo editors and researchers are sitting at a huge illuminated table that lights color transparencies, viewing batches of slides frame by frame. They scrutinize incoming film for focus, color, content, composition, and overall quality. More than 18,000 images compete for space in every issue. Only seventy-five to eighty-five photographs will make the final cut and be published. Of those, between twenty-six and thirty-five will depict the week's foreign news events. A photographer's efforts can often be seen near an editor's feet, in the form of rolls of discarded slides, which lie in cardboard boxes beneath the desk. Those that are selected will be seen by millions, making the publication one of the most influential and powerful media institutions in the world.

Photojournalists negotiate for work in a variety of ways. Established photographers generally prefer to be put "on assignment," which means they get a standard day rate plus their travel expenses for the duration of the assigned story. If this is not possible, prior to shooting a story a photographer may ask the magazine for a "guarantee"—a pledge of money that will at least cover expenditures. In return, the publication gets "first look" at the photographer's rolls of film. If anything is used, an additional sum is agreed upon, with the amount itself determined by how valuable or newsworthy the magazine considers the set of pictures.

Less experienced photographers trying to break into the market will often need to gamble their own money on stories at first and send their material in "on speculation." If they're lucky, something will be published and they'll be paid for the use of that particular image. Over time photographers learn that no matter how much they may enjoy taking pictures, news is a business.

In Jimmy's office, our conversation is continually interrupted. "Where's the Gorbachev take?" "Who do we have in Pakistan?" "Hey, Colton, pick up the line." The atmosphere is casual and chaotic. Irreverent jokes about the latest crisis spread around the room, everyone laughing. As foreign editor, Jimmy understands that news is as transient and unpredictable as the collect calls during all hours of the day and night from anxious photographers informing him of a breaking story, and as volatile as these same photographers, who spend their lives seeing the strangest of human predicaments.

On the wall next to Jimmy's desk is a portrait of Olivier Rebbot, a French photographer who had worked for *Newsweek* in Central America. A humble and decent man, he was one of the few photographers to encourage me when I began shooting. In January 1981, while on assignment for *Newsweek* in El Salvador, he was caught in a crossfire between government troops and guerrilla snipers and badly wounded. He died soon after in a hospital in Miami. The Overseas Press Club of America's prestigious award, "Best Photographic Reporting from Abroad," is named after him.

Over lunch, Jimmy asks if I'd be willing to move to Egypt, which is the one question I've been fearing. The foreign press who work in the Middle East are habitually divided into those who cover the Arab world and those who cover Israel. *Newsweek*, like most major news organizations, has one bureau in Jerusalem and one in Cairo. While a plethora of photographers live in Israel, relatively few are based in Arab countries, primarily because the region itself is so frustrating. Photographers can spend months trying to talk themselves into a visa, not always successfully. Nations like Iraq or Syria often become "newsworthy" simply because a visa is suddenly acquired. If a big story "breaks" and you don't have the proper visa, you're stuck. And as I'd discovered in Libya, the fact that you have a visa doesn't always mean you'll be allowed to take pictures.

If I decide to stay in Israel, it will be a lot tougher to get into Arab countries and I'll run the risk of jeopardizing whatever assignments Jimmy may offer me. Living in Cairo would make more sense, particularly from *Newsweek*'s point of view. But I want to see both sides, to try to understand the Arab world by covering it, and Israel by living there. I explain this to Jimmy, and by the end of the day we come to an agreement. He offers me a retainer, which guarantees me a certain amount of assignment work each month, to cover upcoming or breaking news stories in the Middle East.

And I promise that I will no longer shoot for *Newsweek*'s main competitor, *Time*. We don't sign any papers. The deal is concluded with a handshake and a few hundred rolls of film that will be replenished when necessary.

I know it's not going to be easy. As far as I know, I'll be the only photographer based in Israel whose beat is the entire Arab world. This will most likely cause resentment among the photographers living in Cairo and perhaps the suspicion of those in Israel. All of the photographers and camerapeople working in Israel are either Israeli or married to Israelis, and believe me, I am not welcome in the fold. I was told point-blank by the *Time* photographer, who knew I had a good relationship with *Time*'s photo editor in New York: "We'll see to it you don't work. Move to Cairo. Move to Amman. Move anywhere but here."

So I am aware, at least superficially, that I will be viewed as an outsider. Fortunately, my family name does not give away my heritage, but I'm sure that every time I fill out a visa application and lie about my religion, every time I have to hide my passport with its Israeli stamps, I'll be reminded of two things: my Jewishness and the complexities that underlie Arab-Israeli relations, which defy simplistic representation.

PART 2

The Moment and the Mask

LOCATION/YEAR: JORDAN, KING HUSSEIN'S PRIVATE PLANE,
MOROCCO, CYPRUS; 1985.

Stillness: a portion of time
held motionless. But what, in
fact, had he seen?

—OCTAVIO PAZ

8

His Majesty

(AUGUST 1985)

Fouad Ayoub leans back in his chair, reading a long typewritten report, asserting his authority. I can tell he's not concentrating by the way his eyes flicker around the page. Instead of offering a cup of coffee or tea, he forgoes the traditional amenities of Arab culture, giving the impression of having little time at his disposal. If he aims to make me uncomfortable, he succeeds perfectly.

I sit quietly in his elegant office full of books and papers and telephones and an oil painting of King Hussein, studying this tall, prim man whose perhaps grandiose title is the Royal Palace press liaison. Dressed impeccably in a gray, double-breasted, pinstriped suit and silk tie, his manner is smug and his face is clean-shaven, lacking the thick mustache worn by almost all Arabs. I guess him to be in his mid- to late forties.

When at last he does address me, his voice has the same wintry tone my father so often uses, impatient with an undercurrent that chides. He speaks at length as if he were a college professor, lecturing me about the American media's coverage of the Middle East generally, and Jordan specifically, affecting a Bostonian accent, procured during his year as a Harvard fellow.

Through all of this I stoically smile. Aside from the occasional "photo ops" scheduled for the foreign press, the only way a photographer can photograph the king is if Fouad chooses to arrange it. I begin to think it's hopeless, until the conversation turns to the king's appearance.

"His Majesty shaved off his beard five years ago," Fouad says. His voice becomes indignant as he then informs me that *Newsweek*'s photo-reportage is so outdated that the magazine is still using pictures of the king from the days when he had a full beard.

The claim, however ludicrous, is highly relevant to the tedious game of which we're in the midst, a very oriental process. I plunge into the conversation with a new strategy, conducting a subtle negotiation.

"Fouad, you know we're interested in doing an in-depth profile of the king. After all, he's a key figure in the Middle East peace process, and a major story could be useful. As you've pointed out, it's crucial that Americans understand his and Jordan's pivotal role. But while you're deciding if that's possible, maybe I could attend a few local photo ops and at least take some current head shots of His Majesty so *Newsweek* won't need to resort to out-of-date portraits."

Fouad is quiet for a moment. He knows he's trapped himself, and I enjoy watching him squirm.

"Yes, well," he says, "I suppose it would be a good idea. But if I arrange this type of opportunity for you, then you must promise you won't try to speak to him."

———

The palace camera corps consists of Hussein's personal photographer, a Jordanian television crew, and two local newspaper photographers, all of whom are men. The next day, as I stand alongside the wall squeezed in between them, "His Majesty"—as everyone calls him—walks through the doorway. He is wearing a navy pinstriped suit with a white shirt and dark-blue tie patterned with small light-blue diamonds. His shoulders are wide, his build stocky but athletic, reminding me that he has a black belt in karate and has the reputation of being an ace marksman. There are deep circles under his eyes, and he is balding and graying.

Here in this room inside the Diwan, the name for the Royal Offices, the king will approve the credentials of four new foreign ambassadors. It's the only photo op Fouad has agreed to let me attend. I channel my energies into a single mental flow, determined to send the king a telepathic message.

It must be working—either that or my bright yellow jumpsuit—for between ambassadors the king walks toward me, and now this powerfully built man stands in front of me, his eyes searching my face. Then, in a tone full of humor, as if he has known me for years, the king says, "What are you doing here?"

From the corner of my eye, I see Fouad lurking in the background. "I was hoping to be able to talk to you about that," I whisper.

The king nods briefly, and in that small, seemingly insignificant exchange, a gesture lingers, something instinctive. He returns to his desk to receive the last of the ambassadors.

Fouad is silent as he hustles me out of the Diwan into a Mercedes that will take me back to my hotel. The sun bears down on my skull. The side entrance to the Royal Offices flashes and is thrust open, the sound of voices stirs, and a formidable-looking Bedouin guard, wearing the tan uniform of the Desert Patrol complete with crossed bandoliers and dagger, comes rushing toward us. His Majesty would like to see me now. I turn around and retrace my steps with Fouad hovering closely behind, his expression controlled but furious.

The Diwan is a one-story limestone structure of subdued elegance, and I hasten down the corridor, passing office after office. When finally I see the king framed in the last doorway, it occurs to me that I know nothing about royal protocol.

In my thoughts I struggle to say "Your Majesty" with deference, but the phrase rolls around my tongue with childish impudence. I deliberately chose the yellow jumpsuit for this morning's shoot, and I suddenly wish I'd picked something more dignified and stylish. I find myself at a near trot so as not to keep him waiting, while at the same time hoping to appear calm and ladylike. Do I shake his hand or curtsy, the thought of which conjures up my early teenage years, white gloves, dancing school, and the advent of women's lib. It's all rather absurd, and I begin to giggle. As I near Hussein's office I slow my pace, and fortunately the king takes over.

He smiles warmly. "So, they found you," he says, closing the heavy door to his office, his expression jovial. Standing only an inch or so taller than me, about five feet three, he reminds me briefly of my grandfather. That calm presence, the quiet assurance, and the easygoing manner. We shake hands, and instead of moving to his executive-style desk, he motions me to one of the huge white armchairs arranged around a glass coffee table. He seats himself in the adjacent chair, offers me a cigarette, leans forward to light it, and then takes one for himself so that my first impression is not of his features, but of the lack of formality, as if, at least from the king's point of view, there's nothing out of the ordinary about this unscheduled encounter.

"Now tell me, what really brings you here?" he asks.

It had taken months to convince *Newsweek* that we should develop a relationship with Amman's Royal Palace. I make my little speech, explaining that *Newsweek* is interested in a profile, perhaps for his upcoming fiftieth birthday. His decision made, he clasps his hands across his stomach and says, "So we'll plan to work closely together this week."

I take advantage of the moment to ask him what a typical day is like so that I can begin to think about pictures.

"A typical day? One that never ends, unfortunately. It's the kind of responsibility where it doesn't end at a specific hour. I try to spend as much of the very little time that comes my way with my family and with the children. I've always wanted to give them all the things I never had, all the things I never enjoyed. And those are precious moments. But beyond that, one's continuously involved with what's happening either in Jordan, or in the area, or in the world. So one is always within easy reach of a telephone. I come to work in my office. I don't like that very much indeed. I prefer to be outside with real people whenever I can. There is no set pattern. One tries to catch up with oneself."

There is something almost rueful in his tone, a kind of resignation, and it occurs to me that "His Majesty" is more than an expression. It suggests something about that person's heritage, which is different than talking to a president or prime minister, whose term can be seen as a function, an interval in time. The king belongs to a family that traces its descent to the Prophet Mohammed and to the clan el-Hashem, the oldest house in Arabia.

"Can you ever do that? Catch up with yourself?" I ask, thinking that after all these years, this job of king must be terribly wearying, a kind of life sentence.

Hussein smiles, but it is a forced smile that barely lasts. "I haven't been able to all that much."

He stands up and shows me to the door. His eyes are those of a man at peace with himself. His face is that of a king facing constant battle. "Are you also planning to cover the Arab Summit next week?"

"Yes, I'm supposed to. I believe the plane to Casablanca leaves Sunday."

"Good." He shakes my hand. "Then we'll be seeing quite a lot of each other."

9

Let's Get Some Color

(AUGUST 1985)

On the way back to the hotel, I think about how most of the publications I've worked with are drawn into the outrageous in life's historic moments, news as an extravaganza. Or, I wonder, is it what their public wants? I never could break the code of how editors decide which stories should receive front-page coverage, when events and personalities of equal substance are arbitrarily overlooked or abandoned. Arafat; Qadhafi; Iran's Ayatollah Khomeini; Iraq's Saddam Hussein; Hafez el-Assad of Syria; Hosni Mubarak of Egypt; the Emir of Kuwait; King Fahd of Saudi Arabia; Israeli prime ministers Shimon Peres, Yitzhak Shamir, Yitzhak Rabin, Benjamin Netanyahu; plus Lebanon's exhausting civil wars and vendettas, the strife of modern Israel, the predicament of the Palestinians. All appear on the covers of *Newsweek* and *Time* with uncanny frequency.

How much, I wonder, has the public been misled about the qualities and characteristics of the household names, the people in the news who populate our consciousness? How far is their newsworthiness or notoriety created by the mass media? How much is their image "retouched" by the press corps' latest opinions or personal beliefs? What makes a particular person or country or event newsworthy? And why, when I look at the Middle East's cast of characters, has King Hussein of Jordan been the one personage consistently passed over as a cover story?

He was thrust into the arena nearly four decades ago at the age of sixteen, a soft-spoken, sensitive young Arab, a boy-king whose reign began in 1952, in an era when Harry Truman was still president and Winston Churchill prime minister. He stepped onto a wobbly throne after his father, King Talal, afflicted with schizophrenia since adolescence, was forced to abdicate. A year earlier, he witnessed the murder of his grandfather, King Abdullah, in Jerusalem.

Educated in Britain at Harrow and Sandhurst, King Hussein has ruled longer than any living head of state. He is the only leader who has actually lived through the modern history of the Middle East, not to mention a legion of American administrations to date: Harry S. Truman, Dwight D. Eisenhower, John F. Kennedy, Lyndon Johnson, Richard Nixon, Gerald Ford, Jimmy Carter, and Ronald Reagan. He has been accused of being interested only in keeping his throne and portrayed as a benign dictator. Almost everyone agrees he is a man of principle, but they feel he lacks courage. He has survived bomb threats, an attempted coup, and at least five assassination plots.

In 1958, as he was piloting his plane, two Syrian MiGs attacked him. A skilled pilot, he managed to escape. In 1960, a doctor prescribed nose drops for sinus trouble. Opening a new bottle, a drop fell on the washbasin. He watched as the drop sizzled, then burned a hole through the washbasin—someone had replaced the medicine with sulfuric acid. The king's oldest son, Abdullah, is said to have slept outside his father's bedroom with a gun beneath his pillow to protect him.

I think about the time I photographed the king, during George Shultz's visit to the region in the spring of 1985. They were in Aqaba at the summer palace, on the veranda with their wives. I photographed Shultz walking along the veranda. Then Hussein came out and I asked him to join the Secretary of State and "take a walk." His aides looked at me, horrified, but Hussein was generous about it and strolled down the walkway toward the sea. In the end, *Newsweek* used a picture of Shultz standing alone looking contemplative for a story the following week on the CIA's involvement in a car bombing in Lebanon.

I suspect that the king's character conflicts with media requirements. He is humble, simple, and old-fashioned, incapable of the kind of gestures that precipitate good theater. Since the advent of satellite television, the journalistic ideal of objectivity—"give me the facts"—has been replaced by the seemingly more profound but ultimately cruder "let's get some color." Hussein, who values the rules of decorum, whose demeanor is fundamentally sober and sane, belongs to a generation gone out of style.

10

House of Hashem

(AUGUST 1985)

I wait impatiently in my hotel room to be summoned. Tuesday. Wednesday. Thursday. Friday. Every day I talk to Fouad. Every day it looks worse and worse. Summit coming up, Fouad says. His Majesty's schedule is too busy. Friday afternoon I meet Marcel and Gretty, a young, influential Jordanian couple. I tell them the story. It turns out that they're designing the home of Fouad's cousin. They offer to call Fouad's cousin and exert some social pressure. I decide I have nothing to lose. Saturday, they call him. Sunday morning, Fouad calls me. Stay on standby, he tells me. It will probably happen Monday morning.

On Monday morning I'm summoned. The journalists' plane for Casablanca left yesterday. I ask Fouad if there's any chance I can fly with the king to Casablanca. Fouad says absolutely not. Impossible. His Majesty never takes journalists on his private plane.

At the king's residence, I sit in the living room with Fouad waiting. A Bedouin guard approaches me and takes me to the base of a staircase, where I meet Hussein and Queen Noor. Hussein immediately sends Fouad on an errand.

"What happened to you?" the king asks. "I thought we were going to be working together this week." His voice sounds curious, warm, genuinely confused. Queen Noor is standing with him.

"So did I," I say. "I've been waiting in my hotel room all week."

"And what about the Arab Summit?" he says. "Weren't you planning to cover it?"

"I had planned to, but the only plane from Amman to Casablanca left yesterday."

"We were told that *Newsweek* didn't want you to cover the summit and that you had left," Queen Noor says.

"That's not quite accurate. I was supposed to cover the summit, but given the possibility of a photo session today, and the problem of plane schedules, we made a decision for me to stay here."

"Well, why don't you fly to Casablanca with us tomorrow?" King Hussein says.

"I would love to. Is that a serious invitation?"

The king nods. "Yes. Of course."

"See," Queen Noor says, "now you can have your cake and eat it too!"

His Majesty gives me approximately one hour for a photo session. I photograph him in his office. On the balcony. With Queen Noor. He is formal and stilted, almost embarrassed to be the object of attention. Yet despite this he is thoughtful and courteous. He doesn't rush me, tries to please. He lifts my camera bag, and I can't think of any other head of state who has ever noted the weight of it, much less actually picked it up.

He takes me to the ham radio room, where I take more photographs. He rolls up his sleeves, suddenly relaxed. His call sign: "This is JY One, Hussein on the mike."

"You know, I was the first person to contact the space shuttle when it went up," he says.

"When did you get interested in radios?" I ask.

"Oh, a long time ago I was presented with a station. I've always been interested in electronics. It's a nice way of taking a rest from everything. Being in touch with people who eventually one sometimes meets in different parts of the world. All ages, all kinds of backgrounds. Fortunately no religious topics, no politics. Just human beings in touch with each other."

In the end, the shoot takes place in six locations—the king's private office, his ham radio room, his portico and garden, on his motorcycle just before he zips off to work, and reviewing the Royal Guard outside his office. Creating this series of portraits of Hussein is disturbing to me, for no matter how many pictures I take, no matter how many backgrounds we choose, his personality eludes my attempts to capture it.

Back at the hotel, I order dinner and pack. The king's plane will be leaving early.

In the middle of the night I get a terrible case of food poisoning. I am incredibly sick. At 5 a.m., I call the hotel reception and ask them to send me a doctor. I'm afraid I won't be able to make Hussein's plane. The doctor comes.

"Do whatever you want," I tell him. "I've got to get on that plane.

11

Up, Up, and Away

(AUGUST 1985)

ATTN: JIMMY COLTON/NEWSWEEK PHOTO NY

JIMMY: FLYING WITH KING HUSSEIN TOMORROW TO CASABLANCA FOR

ARAB SUMMIT "EXTRAORDINAIRE." NO OTHER JOURNALISTS INVITED.

HAVE MEANWHILE DEVELOPED DEVASTATING CASE OF FOOD POISONING.

HOPEFULLY WILL MAKE THE PLANE.

I barely make the plane. The interior is exactly the same as any Boeing 727, and I realize I'm childishly disappointed.

I'm still feeling pretty shaky, resting in the back. The next thing I know, King Hussein is standing over me, a worried expression on his face. He asks me if I'm feeling all right.

"Would you mind if I sent my doctor back to look at you?" he says.

I am charmed immediately. I am no longer objective, my opinions about King Hussein already formed, and I remain curious as to why, from an American perspective, he still remains a largely misunderstood figure.

Later I'm summoned to the cockpit, where I find the king, who has a fanatical love of flying, sitting at the control panel.

"How old were you when you started to fly?" I ask.

"Eighteen."

"You remember, I'm sure, your first flight. Were you scared?"

He smiles. "Oh, my first flight was really a very scary one because I believe that the instructor, a very dear friend of mine, was told that he should do everything he could to dissuade me from flying. So he did that, and the first flight was very, very miserable."

"Who told him that?"

"The government, and the late commander of the armed forces, and the Arab leader at the time, Glubb Pasha. I was asked when I wanted to fly again, and I said tomorrow. I somehow got over it and continued. And as you know, I enjoy flying very, very much."

En route, we discuss his attempts over the years to solve "the Palestinian problem." While the king is pushing for dialogue and hoping to get the Arab League to endorse his peace initiative, he knows his efforts are probably doomed from the start.

"I believe," he tells me, "the passage of time has not helped. It has created changes in the occupied territories. It has created greater bitterness. It has created a greater feeling of injustice and growing despair. It has created new realities that unfortunately have put obstacles in the path of a solution."

"How do you define peace?" I ask him.

"Peace is one of justice, of people having their rights recognized, of enjoying those rights. . . . God in his wisdom intended Jerusalem to be the meeting place of not only Muslims, but all of us who have turned toward God and recognized the Almighty. All religions . . . The challenge for mankind throughout history has been for us to realize why Jerusalem is so important for the three great religions—not for them to fight over it. But for them to realize it must become the essence of peace. The meeting place, the symbol of peace, the reality of peace."

ATTN: GWS FROM CAROL/CASABLANCA

DAD: SENIOR MOROCCAN SECURITY SOLDIER OF SOME 6/5 IN STATURE DECIDED TO DEMONSTRATE HIS EVER-READY ROUGH AND TOUGH TACTICS AND TECHNIQUES ON YOUR DIMINUTIVE DAUGHTER. IN NEED OF EQUIPMENT REPLACEMENTS. PLEASE ORDER FOLLOWING AND AIR FREIGHT. WOULD MEAN PROFESSIONAL SALVATION. WILL REIMBURSE. . . .

ATTN: KAREN MULLARKEY/PHOTO

SLUG: KING HUSSEIN PROFILE

KAREN: A FEW RECENT DEVELOPMENTS YOU SHOULD KNOW ABOUT . . . WAS NOT ABLE TO CLEAR PICTURES OUT OF CUSTOMS UNTIL LATE LAST NIGHT. PRESENTED THEM TO HIS MAJESTY THIS AFTERNOON—HE WAS VERY PLEASED. MANY THANKS TO YOU FOR YOUR EFFORTS IN THIS. THE KING AND I HAVE STRUCK UP A RATHER REMARKABLE RAPPORT. HE INVITED ME TODAY TO GO TO AQABA—HIS RESORT RESIDENCE—A FEW DAYS FROM NOW, WHERE I CAN WORK ON A REAL "BEHIND-THE-SCENES"— IN A RELAXED ENVIRONMENT WHERE HE IS NOT CONSTANTLY INTERRUPTED BY OFFICIAL MEETINGS, ETC. . . . IT'S A BEAUTIFUL SETTING AND WILL BE WONDERFUL FOR PIX. IN THE MEANTIME HE HAS OFFERED TO

ARRANGE FOR ME TO PHOTOGRAPH JORDANIAN MILITARY, WHICH IS VERY RARE, AND SOME SPECIAL PIX IF REQUESTED. I HAVE ALSO BEEN GIVEN HIS DIRECT TELEPHONE LINE, AND TOLD I CAN USE IT AT ANY TIME, AND THAT ALL CONTACT FROM NOW ON WILL BE HANDLED DIRECTLY WITH HIM. THIS ALLEVIATES THE PROBLEM I WAS HAVING BEFORE IN GETTING THROUGH TO HIS MAJESTY SINCE I NO LONGER HAVE TO WORK THROUGH THOSE WHOSE JOB IT IS TO KEEP JOURNALISTS AT A DISTANCE FROM HIM. THUS THIS TRIP HAS BEEN EXTREMELY VALUABLE AND I ASSUME YOU WILL BE PLEASED ABOUT THE ABOVE, AND I WILL FINALLY HAVE THE CHANCE TO DO SOME OF THE PICTURES THAT I WOULD REALLY LIKE TO DO. . . . NOV. 11 BY THE WAY IS THE KING'S 50TH BIRTHDAY, SO IT'S PERFECT TIMING FOR MAJOR PROFILE/RETROSPECTIVE . . . ALSO, I ASKED HIS MAJESTY TO AUTOGRAPH A PICTURE FOR YOU—THOUGHT IT WOULD BE NICE FOR YOUR OFFICE. CAROL

12

Private Conversations (I)

King Hussein and I became friends that summer, when he invited me to fly with him to Casablanca. From then on, whenever I passed through Jordan, we would get together for a half hour or so and discuss whatever concerns either of us had at that particular moment. He was always frank, straightforward, and charming. Sometimes I would bring a tape recorder, always remembering the first time I brought one with me and how, with his customary tact, he turned the tape recorder around so that the mike faced in the right direction.

What will always move me most about King Hussein is his trust, his almost naïve candor, so that from the outset I am unable to view him with the kind of distance a news photographer retains when looking at a "subject" through the prism of a lens. He has every reason not to trust anyone. Syrians, Egyptians, Palestinians, Israelis, Americans—all have deceived him, and yet he doesn't stop trying.

For as long as I will know him, I will never find a way to capture his character in a two-dimensional frame. To me, he is a strangely isolated, almost mystical, yet determined individualist. To draw him out, I will have to put down the camera and, in the end, I become more interested in the person than the photographic image.

___

ON THE LOSS OF HIS GRANDFATHER

CS: What do you remember about the day your grandfather was assassinated?

KH: (He is silent for a moment.) You want me to go through the whole experience? I remember it very vividly . . . very vividly. (He is silent again.)

My grandfather was everything to me—a father, an example—who a few days before had asked me a strange question, which I've tried to live up to ever since. He asked me to ensure that his work was not lost and that I would continue to serve the Arab nation and this country as he had done. That particular day, I went with him to the city of Nablus because people insisted that we spend the day with them. We had the intention to go pray at the Al-Aqsa Mosque. I remember being in the uniform that he insisted I wear that morning. It was the only one that I had. I remember the meeting that he had in Jerusalem with certain Palestinians that fateful Friday. I remember him speaking about his relations with some of them. The fact that his differences with people were not of a personal nature, but were matters of policy and approach. I remember him speaking of death and that he wished he would go while he was still in possession of his faculties and the best way in his view would be from a bullet from an unknown assailant.

I remember when we arrived at the mosque, walking in a rather tense atmosphere, surrounded by guards. And I remember him reaching the gate of the mosque and turning around to tell the commander that guards should not salute and create a disturbance in such a holy place. I remember being alongside him, and then dropping back as we prepared to enter.

And then there was a man with a revolver in his hand, pointing at my grandfather. And I remember feeling that time froze, and the bullet, and my grandfather falling. I remember going for the man, or going in his direction, and at the same time, fire breaking out, from inside and outside the mosque. I remember people disappearing. The man falling and firing, and one bullet ricocheting off a medal I had on my chest. And feeling a burn on my ear from a bullet that had been fired not from his direction but from behind me.

And then reaching for my grandfather. Realizing that there wasn't much that could be done. His doctor arriving. I remember undoing his tunic, and that we made a stretcher from a carpet. And one of his chief advisors who had run into the mosque, coming out with blood gushing out of his leg from a wound he had received, and trying to tie it up. And then walking with him toward the hospital.

I remember the anger on the faces of people around us. The madness that prevailed. And I also remember how many of the people who were around him as he entered the mosque had just disappeared.

Those are the memories I have of that day.

———

CS: I want to set aside present-day news and events and bring you back to August 11, 1952—the day you were declared king. What were your thoughts the day it happened?

KH: Well first of all, it was a total and unexpected development. In a very short space of time I saw a tremendous change in my life, in regard to Jordan's monarchy and politics and the region. My grandfather really was a father and friend to me, a man I admired and respected and grew to love very, very deeply. I lived with him for six months, from daybreak till the end of the day. I learned a lot. And then just before I lost him, he wanted me to promise him that I would make sure his work was not lost. I made the promise. I didn't realize what it really would mean.

CS: But you were only sixteen.

KH: I was. So it was really almost overwhelming. In every way, and in every respect.

_____

ON ISRAEL

CS: You're in the position of having to know everything about Israel. Yet you can't go there, or if you could or do, you can't be seen. How do you put together a picture for yourself?

KH: I've always tried to place myself in the position of my opponents. And I've always tried to understand exactly what challenges they face as well as what challenges I do. I've always placed myself on both sides of any problem, in addition to whatever can be gleaned in the way of other information.

CS: Is there an Israeli state of mind, an Israeli national character?

KH: State of mind? Well, I must admit to great disappointment because I couldn't believe that people who have suffered as the Jewish people have suffered would somehow commit the same mistakes and errors against others. This is something that I can't comprehend—or accept. And it really is tragic.

But since the creation of Israel was in itself a reaction against ill-treatment by others around the world, against people treating Jews as second-class citizens, there must be inevitably, in the minds of many, this question: "If that is how we started, how can we treat others the same way we were treated?" On the one hand, if things remain the way they are—if there is no war—in another ten or fifteen years we'll see an Arab population that is almost equal to the Jewish population. Then what happens? The situation itself is a recipe for disaster. Is it foreseeable that Israel will grant these people, even if they annex all these territories, the same political and other rights as Israeli citizens? And if that happens, what happens to the Jewish state?

And on the other hand, if the other school is more dominant—the school that believes in the fortress, and has a fortress mentality—then inevitably they will have to move to expel people and to contribute toward another eruption in this region, only God knows what the results of that will be. And I believe this might explain something we've heard throughout the world in the last few years, the idea or cliché that "Jordan is Palestine." It is as if it was an attempt by some in Israel to suggest that Palestinians have another home somewhere—as if that home was a vacant lot. In other words, Palestinians do not have any rights on their own soil. I don't believe we hear it as much as we used to, but nonetheless it does identify with some elements in Israel that believe in, and will inevitably try, to expel Palestinians from the whole of Palestine. I think probably there is a split among the elder generations of both schools and the younger generation coming up. Naturally one hopes that eventually there will be reasonable and responsible elements who can act in the interests of future generations, who will have the final say.

cs: One of the main obstacles to the Israeli mental state—and I think this pertains to a wide percentage of the population, whatever their beliefs—is that Israelis can't really believe that there will ever be an Arab nation or an Arab people who, in their heart of hearts, will accept them.

kh: I believe it is possible. It's sad that this might not be perceived by some but, . . .

cs: but it's not perceived . . .

kh: This is a big mistake.

cs: It's a big mental obstacle.

kh: Well, I don't believe that Israel can live as an alien creation in that way.

cs: It can't survive as one?

kh: Exactly. Israel must be a part of this area. And this can only happen through peace.

cs: If you had the chance to go to the West Bank for one day, what would you do? Where would you go?

kh: If the conditions were right for me to go there, if there was peace and a solution to the problem, I'd love to go to Jerusalem and visit the tomb of my dead grandfather, and to Al-Aqsa.

cs: Do you think you'll ever be able to go back?

kh: I'm not sure.

cs: If you were the leader of Israel today—if you could step into that role, if you could internalize Jewish fear, Jewish skepticism, Jewish paranoia—how would you act? What would you do, given the situation today?

kh: I would certainly try to look at, again, how future generations would make judgments. I would try to divorce myself and Israel from complexes and fears of the past, and realize that there is an opportunity to contribute toward a change. Israel cannot continue indefinitely to live as a fortress—with nuclear weapons, or with whatever, as a means of surviving indefinitely. I would try to resolve the problem of its neighbors, particularly the Palestinians, and the problems of its relations with the entire area, in terms of a comprehensive peace that would mean a bright future for Israelis and others alike.

ON THE UNITED STATES

cs: Are you among those who believe that only the superpowers can impose a solution in the Middle East?

kh: No. No, I don't believe that they can, but I believe that they can contribute toward it very, very much indeed. And obviously the superpowers can contribute toward it more if they were to assume their responsibilities as superpowers. Not to be the backers of one side or another but to act on principles and to act on applying those principles equally in the Arab-Israeli issue, as in other issues in the world.

Unfortunately what has happened with the United States is that it has lost a lot of its credibility on the Arab side because it's not neutral. And the feeling here, in this part of the world, is that the American public does not really know what is happening in this area. What we have sought is to identify with what we're trying to uphold throughout our struggle. There is much in common between us. But unfortunately, they are not informed. They are not aware. And therefore, they do not apply the principles for which they stand to this conflict. And that's why we have suggested time and again, that if there is a solution, the United States can play a role, and a very, very important role, but maybe the solution should be sought within the context of the five permanent members of the Security Council—to avoid polarization between the superpowers, and to help the parties to the conflict achieve peace.

------

cs: Do you have a dream, a vision, that lies behind and motivates your search for peace?

KH: To give generations to come a chance to live in a different world than that which has been outlined. To give them a chance to live with human dignity and with peace and security. To give them the chance to divert their energies and resources toward creating a better kind of world, and influencing the rest of the world in a positive way. It is really my dream to contribute toward that—this has been my goal, as it was my grandfather's before me.

cs: Is it lonely at times? To try and attain a goal that involves the participation of those who might not share your dream. It often cuts a very lonely path.

KH: There are times when the questions, the internal turmoil, have to be masked. And in a time of crisis, you have to have a smile. So one has to unfortunately live with a façade at times. But I mean, if we are human, we have feelings, obviously.

ON RELIGION

cs: Is there some sort of ongoing regional contest to capture the will of the Muslim people?

KH: From within the area or from outside?

cs: From within the area.

KH: Well, if you look at Israel, and you see more extreme attitudes developing, you'll probably see a reaction to it on the Arab side. If it is an extreme religious fanatical approach, you'll find something similar developing as a reaction to it.

But basically speaking, I do not believe that much of what we have seen or lived through in the recent past, or continue to live through in the way of acts and actions in the name of faith and religion, really has anything to do with religion or faith. They are usually a guise for either those who are trying to achieve goals of dominance, or maybe it's part of a bigger game in this world. But it certainly is not faith or religion.

cs: So is there a "who" that's behind it?

KH: I believe in many cases there is a who that's behind it.

cs: Well, specifically who is behind it now?

KH: I believe it is very, very difficult to define who is behind it, but I'm sure that it is part of a bigger plan in this world.

cs: If what you are saying is possible, then it makes the situation much more frightening.

kh: It does. But as far as we are concerned, what is most upsetting is that we are witnessing an approach to try to turn the clocks back and to act in a spirit which is entirely different to that of our religion and faith. And certainly the acts of violence that result in divisions in this area between Muslims, let alone between believers, is so alien to everything that we believe in, that what is happening represents a threat to the Arab order.

––––––––

ON LIFE, LOVE, FAMILY

cs: What do you love deeply in this world?

kh: People. I love people. I love the earth. And I am interested in everyone I've had contact with.

cs: What makes you laugh?

kh: What makes me laugh? Not very much. (He laughs.) It's sad sometimes. I'm so involved in problems, and the resolution of these problems, that you discover that laughter is not a habit anymore.

cs: You have eleven children—is that right?

kh: A total of twelve, with my adopted daughter.

cs: And they range in age from?

kh: From thirty-something to two years . . .

cs: You said those were precious moments, the time you're able to spend with your family . . .

kh: Especially now that they are growing up.

cs: How many are at home?

kh: At home . . . six.

cs: How would you describe the time you are able to spend with them? How do you think they view you as a father?

kh: I spend some very interesting times with them. I suppose it differs with their ages in a way. But they all love each other, and I love them equally. And I'm proud of them. And the nicest moments, in a way, occur with the younger ones who come and sit around and want to know about me, and about what I do, and about this country, and the family, and so on. And I am impressed with their interests and questions.

cs: What do you tell your children about the Arab-Israeli conflict?

kh: I do not tell them anything that is not factual, and that I haven't lived and experienced. And I believe that what I tell them time and again is my hope that efforts will succeed and achieve for all of us in our region a just solution—a solution that future generations can accept and live with. Something that will mean security. It's got to be a solution that recognizes the rights not only of Israel, but also of the Palestinians and of the Arabs to live in peace in this area.

cs: What are your favorite hobbies? Sports?

kh: In sports, I enjoy tennis at the moment. I enjoy the sea whenever I can. Swimming. I like water sports. And I enjoy skiing whenever I can. And I've taken more to that in recent years.

cs: Do you believe that physical discipline augments one's mental discipline?

kh: Yes, I do. And I do exercise at home as well, regularly. And I enjoy flying.

———

ON HIS MEDIA IMAGE

cs: Does your internal self-image differ from, or resemble, what you perceive as your media image?

kh: It depends. What's my media image?

cs: How do you see your own media image?

kh: I think it has generally been all right. I take exception at times to suggestions that—you know, by some—that he's looking after himself, he's looking after his throne. . . . What throne, what self? I mean, I am just an ordinary person trying to do my best for people, for the future. Nothing more. I believe that the fault of many, not only in this part of the world but maybe the world over, is that they feel the world begins and ends with them. I've seen that. I suffered it in terms of people whom I've loved and admired and respected very, very much indeed. . . . As a Hashemite, I have a far more important position as a descendent of the Prophet in the Arab and Muslim world than being the king of Jordan. That's always been my belief.

cs: Every child dreams of what it would be like to be a king. What do you dream of being, other than a king?

kh: I suppose after all these years, it's difficult to have many dreams. But to be a person who basically lives a normal life in a happy environment with everyone around enjoying peace and dignity and the chances to develop and evolve and move ahead.

———

CS: How aware are you of your own mortality?

KH: Well, I've always known that there will come a time when it will all end. But I have never really thought about it. I decided never to think of it on the day I lost my grandfather. Life and death is not in our hands. And there have been so many questions throughout my political life as to the future of myself or Jordan. I've always thought that you have to live with yourself. That was the most important thing. Not time. Do all you can. Do the best that you can. And leave the rest to the Almighty. It's a question of, when it comes, it comes.

CS: How do you look on fear?

KH: Fear is something one has to live with, and it's a part of our being, of course. You fear God, you fear yourself, you fear your own errors, you fear something that confronts you at times. It's something you've got to live with and be able to overcome. I mean for me, a fear of not being able at any point in life to live with myself—for having let people down, for having not done my best—is really something that keeps me awake at night sometimes.

CS: How does one judge their success or failure?

KH: Well, take my case. You know many people have sometimes called me a survivor, or one who survives. . . . But you survive to do something. And in the final analysis, whether I succeed or fail, it's how much I have been able to help the people I'm honored to serve. But even then, the question of just making progress, if you are fortunate enough to have the right elements and ingredients surrounding your life and the lives of those you serve, that in itself is not the ultimate thing. As far as I'm concerned, success or failure is . . . what will people say of us long after? Have we succeeded in giving them a beginning on the right path toward peace and security and a better future?

CS: When history looks back at you, what would you like to be remembered for? What do you hope to be remembered for?

KH: I'd like to be remembered as a person who never dealt with problems on a personal basis or let personal considerations affect his judgment, or cloud them in any way. I'd like to hopefully be remembered as a person who's been honest and sincere. And as one who has tried to contribute toward the establishment of a just and durable peace and a better future for generations to come.

PART 3

Passing Through

LOCATION/YEAR: ISRAEL, CYPRUS, LEBANON,
JORDAN, EGYPT, YEMEN; SUMMER/FALL 1985

If your pictures aren't
good enough, you
aren't close enough.
—ROBERT CAPA

13

TWA Flight #847

(JUNE/JULY 1985)

"Shit."

We were about to have dinner. Linguine with white clam sauce, garlic bread, tomato salad with fresh basil and real imported Parmesan cheese, a bottle of chilled verdicchio. Curtis Wilke of the *Boston Globe* had spent the better part of the afternoon kneading, rolling, chopping, slicing, grating, and simmering things. I have just put the meal on the table when the phone rings.

He slams down the receiver and slips into a torrent of obscenities that terminate with a heavily Mississippi-accented "G-a-w-d-dammit." Among the Jerusalem-based foreign journalists, Curtis's unmistakable, and often incomprehensible, southern twang and gourmet Italian dishes are legendary. Whenever he travels, it seems he somehow manages to detour through Rome, arriving back with a suitcase full of gastronomical delights that simply aren't available in Israel.

"What's wrong?" I'm anxious to eat before the linguine gets cold.

"A fuckin' plane's been hijacked." Curtis pours himself a glass of wine and heads back to the phone. "A TWA flight out of Athens. Looks like it's gawna land in Beirut."

His face is grim, the meal forgotten. In this part of the world neither food nor traveling can be taken for granted, particularly on a Friday night, which is the beginning of the Sabbath. To cover the story we have to find a way out of Israel. Ben-Gurion Airport is virtually shut down, and the Allenby Bridge is closed until Sunday. Fortunately for me, there are a handful of American journalists based here, Curtis among them, whose newspapers are big enough to have a Middle East correspondent but not large enough to have two separate bureaus. Therefore, they have budgets to move around when necessary. Curtis talks to another reporter, who is organizing a chartered plane to Cyprus.

"You interested?" he asks me.

"Yeah, count me in."

"You better go get some sleep. We'll be leaving at 4:30 in the morning. I'll swing by and pick you up."

I drive home, already packing in my mind.

———

I rise before dawn, lightheaded, the scent of jasmine wafting about. My sheets and blankets are crumpled over the edge of the bed. My skin is cold, my face flushed. I reach for a blanket, wrapping its scratchy warmth around my shoulders. It's just past four. A pale blue-gray mist curtains the morning landscape. The voice of a muezzin drifts across the valley.

It is now 4:20 a.m. I go outside and stand at the edge of the curb with my camera bags and suitcase and wait for Curtis. The street is deserted.

At 5 a.m., five of us assemble in the dimly lit departure hall at Ben-Gurion Airport. After our bags have been checked by security, we're whisked up one flight of stairs, down another, out a back door to the runway, and over the tarmac to the small plane we've chartered. At times like this, my two small duffel bags are easier to carry than a large, cumbersome suitcase, especially with a camera bag balanced on each shoulder, when there are no porters around.

The flight to Cyprus is only forty minutes, but there is plenty of time for us to talk about the dangers of continuing on to Beirut Airport, where the hijacked plane, whose passengers were destined originally for Rome, has landed. It has been refueled, and seventeen women and two children have been permitted to leave. The two gunmen aboard are threatening to blow up the aircraft, which is surrounded by Shiite militiamen. Over the last sixteen months, thirteen Westerners have been kidnapped in Lebanon—eight of them American. Everyone's hoping that in the inevitable deluge of journalists for this story, the foreign press will be left alone, at least until the crisis has ended. By the time we land in Larnaca, TWA Flight #847 has already left Beirut and is on its way to Algeria. The nineteen hostages were flown to Cyprus, where they are staying in a hotel.

I go to work immediately. Hopping into a taxi with Curtis, we speed downtown. I scurry and snap the ex-hostages' haggard, sleepless faces, ruthlessly ignoring their anguish for husbands who are still on the plane. I must get them on film before they're put on a U.S. military flight to Paris for debriefing.

While they're worrying about the fate of their family, I'm worrying about an esoteric series of steps and deadlines. There's no time to airfreight film for this particular story, which could be a last-minute cover. In cases like this, we must use the facilities of one of the three major wire services, who transmit pictures to magazines and newspapers around the world.

To wire a photograph, an 8 x 10 print is wrapped around the drum of a machine called a picture transmitter. The transmitter has an optical head that reads the image as the drum revolves and transforms it into sound signals, which are delivered over the telephone line. This is read by a picture receiver, which translates the electronic frequencies into light again and simultaneously gives you back the image. A black-and-white photograph takes fifteen minutes to send, but in a real hurry, the transmitter can be put on double-speed, and the picture wired in exactly seven and a half minutes.

Fortunately, the Associated Press (AP) has a bureau in Cyprus, and a few hours later I'm standing in a pitch-black room, carefully threading two rolls onto stainless steel reels and dropping them into a developing tank. Once the film is processed and dry, I turn on the light box so I can examine the negatives closely with a magnifying lens or loupe. Since the publication won't have the actual rolls of film, both content and layout must be considered. I choose a vertical portrait of two distressed-looking faces and a horizontal shot of the entire group holding hands before they leave for Paris. I notch the two images with a small punch on the edge of the negative strip so the AP photographer will know which frames I want printed. While he goes into the darkroom, I type out three lines of caption information for each photograph to be affixed to the side of the print, then I telex my editor to let him know the pictures will be arriving shortly.

In places where there is no bureau, a wire photographer must bring a complete portable darkroom and the picture transmitter, in addition to the camera equipment that magazine photographers take on location. The hotel room becomes an office and the bathroom doubles as a darkroom. All in all, there is about 180 pounds of gear to lug around. Everything is packed in two or three heavy metal cases, except for the transmitter, which is carried on the plane in its own box because it's so fragile.

By the time my second photograph is wired, the hijacked plane has landed on the runway in Algiers, where another group of women and children are released. Not knowing what else to do, I take a taxi to the seaside hotel where most of the press corps in Cyprus are gathered and, like everyone else, follow the events through the BBC radio.

The terrace outside is full. Reporters, mostly male, from *Time*, *Newsweek*, the big American newspapers, the British dailies, and the television networks cluster around tables, rapping about the skyjacking.

Throughout the night and into the next day, we try to piece together snatches of information from the reports and radio broadcasts being filed by the various reporters who are in Algeria and Lebanon already. The TWA pilot flies back to Beirut during the evening, aware of the danger yet somehow maintaining his cool. One of the two hijackers—who are young Lebanese Shiite Muslim extremists—was holding a live grenade beside the flight control panel. Fear keeps everyone awake as the terrorists walk down the aisles demanding to see each passport, but the passengers are subdued.

Then an American is executed, his body thrown onto the tarmac. Beneath a quiet moon, for it is past midnight, Shiite militiamen secure the runway, allowing more armed gunmen to get on the aircraft, while at least five Americans with "Jewish" surnames are forced off and taken captive somewhere in the darkness of Beirut.

The plane leaves Lebanon before dawn, doubling back to Algeria again, the crisis unfolding under a blazing North African sun. Several passengers collapse from the heat. The cabin reeks and the bathrooms overflow. The hijackers once more threaten to blow up the plane unless hundreds of Shiites are freed from an Israeli prison camp. They threaten to kill the eight Greeks aboard unless another Lebanese Shiite is released from Greek custody and flown across the Mediterranean to join them.

The terrorists seem to be professional. For hours they wait, shrewdly orchestrating international blackmail. When the Shiite who had been detained in Greece suddenly materializes on the runway in Algiers, they release the rest of the women and children and a couple of men. Then they return to Lebanon. By late Sunday night, the remaining thirty or so male passengers are hustled off the plane to Beirut, where they continue to be held hostage. Only the pilot and two crewmen remain on board the aircraft, which is now under the vigilant guard of a bevy of militiamen.

Newsweek tells me to stay in Cyprus. Having decided they don't want an American photographer prowling through the Shiite neighborhoods of Beirut, they've put photographers with other nationalities on assignment there. Their decision, I think, is absurd given the number of American TV crews and reporters who are in Lebanon already, but at least I'm not alone. All of the major networks and media organizations have quadrupled the number of people working on coverage. While most of the press corps are in Beirut, where the actual story is taking place, at least one-third remain in Larnaca, where communications are better. CBS television, with the largest contingent of anyone, has at least twenty people at each location. If any more hostages are released, in all probability they'll be flown here, since it's easy to get from Cyprus to Lebanon.

The next morning, I find myself racing to Larnaca's marina. In a gesture of reciprocation to the Greek government, the hijackers have freed a well-known Greek singer, his female companion, and a Greek American teenager. As they step off the boat we descend, thrusting microphones and cameras at them from all sides, all of us, in our hunter's uniforms and armed with our weaponry, trying to elbow a way to the front of this frenzy. I'm too small to see over anybody's shoulders and instinctively push to the head of the swarm. What's astonishing is not only the aggression, but also how we photographers find ourselves rising to new levels of aggression in order to compete. It doesn't matter who we hit or shove out of the way, our thoughts are only of the scene. And we can't be polite or gentle in such situations. As everyone else bunches up alongside and behind me, I'm suddenly gazing into the singer's stunned eyes, his bearded face only inches away. I'm so close I must use an extra wide-angle lens that will most likely make him look distorted. Our behavior is so unruly that the American Embassy official escorting them shouts: "You all are worse than the fucking terrorists. Now get back. You're like a bunch of animals."

A few hours later, a rumor circulates that another person has been released. We dash to the airport in a convoy of taxis and cluster on the tarmac, cluttering up the area with our equipment. All eyes are on the sky. Before the plane has even touched down, the huge red characters of Lebanon's national carrier, MEA, come into telephotographic view. A photographer's mind is shaped by the kind of images the magazine looks for, the picture editors want and expect. Long shots first: the weary, middle-aged American being escorted down the ramp of the aircraft by Embassy officials. Close-range wide-angles next: focusing on his disheveled appearance, shaky stance, filthy clothing, and horror-stricken expression. And finally the tight shots as he stands in front of us, giving a short statement to the press: his red, swollen eyes, which we all shoot rapidly as they suddenly brim with tears. His son is one of the passengers still held captive. He must find us diabolical and disgusting. But none of us consider the brutality of what we're doing, there's so much pressure on us to get these images.

_____

The unedited television footage of a press conference held at Beirut Airport toward the end of the week really brings it home to me. Five hostages have been brought before some 150 representatives of the world press, ostensibly to establish that the thirty-nine captives are still alive and being treated well. The hostages are sitting at the front of the room, bordered by throngs of young, Kalashnikov-carrying men from "Amal," one of the many militias fighting for control of Lebanon. Although they are not from the same fanatic faction as the "fundamentalist" hijackers, they are clearly co-operating with them, most of the hostages now being under Amal's "protection" in the Shiite strongholds of Beirut.

The photographers and cameramen are shouting and shoving from the beginning of the news conference, disregarding the wild-eyed glare of the gunmen as they vie for the best angles. Some scramble onto a conference table, knocking over beverages and stepping on sweets that had been laid out by the Amal in what is almost a parody of Arabic hospitality. When melee erupts, many of the reporters duck behind chairs while the photographers continue to push even closer to the action in order to capture the strained, clenched expressions on the hostages' faces. The gunmen whisk the hostages out of the room, to be returned only after a barrier of chairs has been set up by the Amal to safeguard the hostages from the press.

———

I pack my film and take it to the airfreight office to send to *Newsweek*. Under normal circumstances, when you work for one of the weekly American news magazines, color film should be in their office by Thursday evening, Friday morning at the latest if it's a major story. The film is sent to the in-house lab for processing upon arrival. Then it has to be edited. Once the story's ready to be laid out, on Friday afternoon or evening, a carousel of potential "selects" is shown to senior writers and editors in the viewing room, where most of the pictures published will be chosen.

I know that none of my photographs will be used for this week's issue. The few rolls I've taken don't have militiamen pointing guns or hijackers holding walkie-talkies, wearing slit-eyed, sinister-looking blue hoods. They aren't terrifying, dramatic, or interesting enough. They cannot compete with the touching sentimentality of the family reunions held all over America for the hostages who have been released, nor of the churchgoing relatives praying for the rest of the hostages' safe return. They won't cause the kind of anger that sweeps the nation during the emotional funeral of U.S. Navy diver Robert Dean Stethem, and none can carry a caption such as one *Newsweek* photo: "The body dumped in Beirut: the killers meant business."

———

Toward the end of the second week, one more hostage is released. This time I flaunt my magazine's name, begging the American Embassy official for at least one picture away from the crowd. At the top of my caption envelope I write "EXCLUSIVE." I want *Newsweek* to know I'm working hard, even though what I enclose is a ridiculously absurd image: "Jimmy Dell Palmer (from Little Rock, Ark.) drinks his first American-made Coca-Cola in the VIP lounge at Larnaca airport after being freed earlier in Beirut today because of a heart condition."

The following day, I have another exclusive—a picture of Olga Conwell, wife of hostage spokesman Allyn Conwell. NBC's *Today* show had sent a Lear jet to Corfu to fetch her, but they were too late. She'd already been snatched up by ABC's *Good Morning America*.

ABC has its headquarters at a hotel in downtown Larnaca where its anchor, Pierre Salinger, has moved in, with Davidoff cigars flown in from Paris. The money being tossed about on this story is as awesome as is the battle for ratings. Aside from MEA, the only planes flying in and out of Beirut regularly are half a dozen television charters unloading a sackful of videocassettes. This week the three major American networks are talking about constructing their own satellite earth stations in Cyprus.

CBS has taken over the mezzanine of my hotel, turning its conference rooms into editing suites. Whenever I walk through the door to try to find out the latest happenings, a staffer instantly sweeps me aside. Voices slide into whispers, hissing at each other to shut up, shut up, as if I might endanger whatever exclusives are being set up in Beirut. Outside the hotel, I can sometimes spot men, CBS staffers, looking down over the beach from the mezzanine terrace, peering into binoculars at two long-legged, topless blonde beauties, Swedish tourists who have become the talk of the hotel and the objects of a series of dare-you-to-do bets, reminding me that this is also the Isle of Aphrodite. And that boys will be boys.

In the effort to out-scoop each other, the networks are bidding for hostage exclusives. Some say cash is actually changing hands. The only network being handed regular exclusives is ABC, whom everyone has begun calling Amal Broadcasting Company. Desperation takes the form of "how do you feel" interviews of family. The battle for ratings is so horrific that eventually the Shiites tack a bulletin in the Commodore Hotel, where most of the press corps in Beirut are staying, stating that "all footage of the hostages should be pooled."

As the hostage crisis continues, those of us in Cyprus increasingly find ourselves bystanders, outside the perimeters of the inside story. Nevertheless almost every morning footsteps can be heard running across the lobby as rumors percolate through the hotel that someone has been freed.

There's so little for us to do here that no one dares to be left behind. We blast off to the airport, loitering on the tarmac for hours like drifters waiting for the wheel of fortune to complete its spin. After forty minutes or so, everyone can be seen sitting or lying around on the runway smoking cigarettes, the sun burning our faces, cameramen casually stripped down to the waist in the Mediterranean heat.

By the end of the second week, I'm worried about not having a Syrian visa. It becomes clear that if the hostages are to be released, it will most probably take place in Syria.

Jimmy calls to tell me to go to Damascus, just in case.

ATTN: ROD NORDLAND/NEWSWEEK URGENT
SHERATON HOTEL DAMASCUS
ROD: ARRIVING DAMASCUS 2030 TONIGHT ON SYRIAN AIR #RB454 DEP. CY-
PRUS 1910. CAN SOMEONE MEET ME AT AIRPORT? DO NOT HAVE VISA. PLS
REPLY SOONEST, SPENCER.

ATTN: ROD NORDLAND/NEWSWEEK URGENT
SHERATON HOTEL DAMASCUS
ROD: TRIED BOARD PLANE TO DAMASCUS LAST NIGHT WITHOUT VISA BUT
TURNED AWAY BY SYRIAN AUTHORITIES WHO REMAINED RESOLUTE. IS
THERE ANY WAY YOU CAN HELP? PHOTO WANTS ME IN. AWAITING REPLY
. . .

It turns out I'm not the only one who's having visa problems. I have dinner with a CBS vice president who, puffing on a cigar, his soft face utterly shocked, says, "I guess they didn't understand who we are."

PRO SPENCER FROM NORDLAND
EYE M IN MERIDIEN HOTEL, DAMASCUS—NOT SHERATON—WHICH WHY
HAVE NOT GOT YOUR MESSAGES TILL NOW. TELL PHOTO TO TRY AND STAY
IN TOUCH WITH NEWSDESK ON PEOPLE'S WHERABOUTS. AM TOLD ARE
NUMBER OF PHOTOGS AND OTHERS IN DETENTION AT DAMASCUS AIRPORT
WHO TRIED TO GET IN VISALESS. SYRIAN GOVT MAY DECIDE TO LET THEM
IN EVENTUALLY, OR THEY MAY JUST DETAIN AND DEPORT, WHO KNOWS
HOW LONG. HOSTAGES EXPECTED LATE THIS AFT.
IF IS PLANE TONIGHT, OR IF HOSTAGES DO NOT ARRIVE, SUGGEST YOU
GIVE IT ANOTHER TRY. ANOTHER POSSIBILITY IS TO FLY BEIRUT AND TAKE
CAR ON BEIRUT-DAMASCUS HIGHWAY. AT THE SYRIAN BORDER CROSSING
JOURNALISTS ARE BEING ALLOWED IN VISALESS. SHOULD YOU DECIDE TO

TRY THAT, CONTACT OUR BUREAU IN BEIRUT FOR INFO ON EXACTLY HOW
TO DO. TAKES 3 HOURS AND SHOULD NOT BE DONE AFTER DARK. RGDS,
NORDLAND.

Fortunately, it's too late. The hostages are already on their way to Damascus for release, and I'm not about to tackle Beirut on my own, trailing half a day behind a convoy of hired press cars following the convoy of hostage victims. I may be a lunatic, but I'm not crazy.

———

On the flight back to Jerusalem, I think about how the hijackers got exactly what they wanted. They terrorized a nation, pressuring the United States to force Israel to release the Lebanese detainees. They were the focus of the world for almost three weeks, with the people they held hostage espousing their cause on national television. We let them get away with it and, more importantly, played into their hands, publishing pictures of freed Lebanese detainees greeting their families, the media equating both situations.

The terrorists have also managed to make Israel appear at least partly responsible for the crime of kidnapping. *Newsweek* points out in its second story on the crisis (July 1, 1985) that "What disturbs American Jewish leaders is that the coverage of the hijackers' demands—and the hostages' gunpoint television appearance—seemed somehow to shift responsibility for the crime at least partly onto Israel." A story on ABC's *Good Morning America* features the families of the imprisoned Shiites as if, some Jews charge, they can be equated with the families of innocent American hostages. An NBC report suggests that "the slain Navy diver Robert Stethem had died in a war begun by the Israeli invasion of Lebanon." Ironically, in the same issue, *Newsweek* runs a photo showing prison detention center tents with a caption that says "Israel's side of the chessboard: The Atlit prison camp where roughly 570 Shiites are held" (July 1, p. 18).

For me, this type of situation is a professional dilemma. The media is being used as a conduit for the kidnappers' demands. Photo-documentation reportage turned into photo-fiction, small visual dramas with staging, composition, and scripting determined by terrorists. The hostages were divided into those who made good spokesmen (the "lead actors") and those who should remain in the background (the "extras").

I click and snap but there is a low murmur growing louder in my head as I work. The quietness of my mind is gone. Framing is not so simple anymore.

14

Exile

(SEPTEMBER/OCTOBER 1985)

This morning I study a photograph of a woman killed yesterday in Larnaca, Cyprus. It was Yom Kippur, the Jewish Day of Atonement. The picture was taken from the pier of the marina by a friend of mine. The woman's body half stands, half dangles, at the edge of a small yacht, her head and upper torso draped across the bow's railing, blood spattering down her arms and hands, spilling onto the deck in between her feet. The picture is as gruesome as the story.

The woman's husband and their friend, not in the frame, also lie dead, shot in the head after being shackled to the lower deck. When they gave themselves up to Cypriot authorities, the three gunmen, two Palestinians and one Briton, raised their hands in triumph. They had murdered one Israeli each. The PLO promptly denied involvement but later, when it was confirmed the guerrillas were members of Force 17, Yasser Arafat's elite commando bodyguard unit, the PLO changed their story, claiming the dead Jewish tourists were Israeli spies.

———

The following week, a squadron of Israeli F-15 fighter jets soar across the Mediterranean skies to Tunisia, 1,500 miles from Tel Aviv. Their bombing of PLO headquarters, including Yasser Arafat's offices at Hamman Shatt on the Gulf of Tunis, is swift and efficient.

It's not the first time the Israelis have tried to assassinate the PLO leader, who survives the attacking war planes, but sixty-three Palestinians and ten Tunisians die, many buried and dozens of others injured by buildings that collapse.

The UN Security Council condemns the Israeli air strike. The vote is 14–0, with one abstention: the United States. I abhor America's silence, the deliberate lack of acknowledgment that the act Israel has committed is an act of state terrorism. The silence legitimizes the violence and ignores the consequences. It reinforces the Individual State as terrorist, while condemning the individual victims of the bombing. What happened to our democratic values? The belief that we should protect fundamental human rights?

And where will the dead be buried? A journalistic question, for I now have to cover the funeral of the sixty-three Palestinians killed in the attack. Their corpses ultimately have to be flown 1,600 miles from Tunisia to Jordan, the only country that has offered to allow its soil to be used as a final resting place for the bodies of the dispossessed. Is this what exile means? That even the dead are not at home?

I stand at a military airstrip in Jordan watching the simple wooden crate-like coffins being carried off the plane, one by one. Israel has claimed the victims of the bombings were all PLO terrorists, but a number of caskets are those of small children.

It is nearly pitch-black when the funeral begins in the outskirts of Amman. I am the only outsider there, and I watch men in a procession shoulder more than five dozen wooden coffins, each one wrapped in the Palestinian flag and a wreath of flowers. A full moon floods the rows of rough-cut tombstones, turning the soil of the burial place golden. Tens of thousands of Palestinians line the rim of the mass grave, anger and anguish engraved on their faces. I see Abu Jihad standing alone amid the multitudes quietly weeping, but before I can make my way toward him, I am swept into the crowd of mourners, many of whom carry framed portraits of a son, a father, a brother.

I see tears all around me. Even though I'm there, I know the pictures won't be used, that this whole event is invisible. In that lightning moment when I click the shutter, I believe this is the real picture. I surrender myself to their sorrow, their struggle. My mind blots out the past, the future. Only the present moment exists.

I cling to my cameras, to this irrelevant work in the face of life and death, to my images of their reality, a grotesque series of ultra-rapid exposures. I photograph the bodies being lowered into the deep black pits, casket after casket swathed in moonlight, and the PLO flags that have come to symbolize home, an identity in exile, a cliché.

And then there is nothing left but crying, a collective wail that erupts in the darkness and returns in my sleep. Of everything I've photographed, these pictures will haunt me the most.

15

Cruising

(OCTOBER 1985)

ATTN: JIM COLTON/NEWSWEEK PHOTO NY

FROM: CAROL SPENCER/RM. 1114 MERIDIAN HOTEL, CAIRO

SLUG: ACHILLE LAURO SEAJACKING

JIMMY: TRANSMITTING EXCLUSIVE PHOTO COLOR OF MRS. KLINGHOFFER

VIA REUTERS SINCE AP REFUSED TO HELP. SHOULD REACH NY IN A FEW

HOURS. BEST RGDS, CAROL

I'm sitting in the bar at the InterContinental in Jordan with three British journalists. It's ten in the evening on October 7. David, a television correspondent for ITN, switches on the BBC World Radio Service and holds his nine-band Sony to his ear.

"Shh. Quiet." He turns the volume up and places the radio on our table, the expression on his face taut as the Beeb tersely announces that the Italian cruise liner *Achille Lauro* was hijacked off the coast of Egypt and its passengers taken hostage. There are no further details and this lack of information creates anxious curiosity. Where's the boat headed now? How many passengers does it have? What's their nationality? Are the hijackers Arab? Why would anyone hijack an Italian cruise ship? Are there any Jews on board? What about Americans? How are we going to cover the story? We stay awake listening to the Beeb on the hour and checking the wires for updates, growing tense and weary, until we assemble the outline of what's happened, a few frail facts.

The *Achille Lauro* set out from Genoa, Italy, six days earlier in perfect cruising weather. The 748 passengers, who were mainly elderly and of many nationalities, looked forward to a leisurely voyage, calm sailing, and steady Mediterranean sunshine. After anchoring at Alexandria, a popular

Egyptian destination, most of the passengers went ashore to see the pyramids. Those who didn't continued on to Port Said, the gateway to the Suez Canal, where the other passengers would rejoin them later. But ten nautical miles out to sea from Alexandria, the leisure ship was commandeered by gunmen and the passengers and crew on board taken hostage.

Throughout the night and into the next day, planes chartered by TV stations are flying over the eastern Mediterranean in every direction as cameramen try to get pictures of the 23,629-ton *Achille Lauro*, which steams along the coast of Syria, detours toward Lebanon, veers off toward Libya, and doubles back again toward Cyprus. Bleary-eyed, I trudge off to the airport with the British television crew and climb into the extra seat of the plane they have chartered in pursuit of a story I can barely imagine. Our destination is Egypt, where the passengers who had inadvertently escaped from the luxury cruise liner are now stranded. With the situation still unfolding, the identity and number of the hijackers unknown, and the ship zigzagging on an unforeseeable sea course, the only thing I'm sure of is that this week's crisis will be next week's cover story.

By mid-morning I'm in the lobby of Cairo's Concorde Hotel, where the hundreds of passengers have been gathered. They sit huddled on the sofas, floor, and even the stairwell, their faces dazed and tearful, their vacation ruined. Others linger in front of the television in the lobby watching the news, which tells them nothing about the scene on board the boat.

My assignment, though not actually difficult, is dismal. As I mix with the various groups, I explain that *Newsweek* is looking for any photographs that were taken on the ship. I try to convince people that their film may be important, perhaps even crucial, particularly if it identifies anyone who is being held hostage at this moment. I speak firmly but gently, promising that all film will be returned as soon as the crisis is over.

I don't say that the magazine hopes to get its hands on photographs of potential victims. It doesn't take long to discover I'm not the only one scavenging for these images, trying to figure out ways to hone raw reality into the magazine's glossy format. At least two photographers have been here before me.

I label the few rolls I've managed to collect so *Newsweek* will know who the film belongs to. Since there's nothing else I can do to illustrate the story, I photograph the abandoned tourists, writing down detailed caption information about a group portrait: Pearl Rosenthal (green and white pantsuit); Frank Hodes (tan pants and jacket); Charlotte Spiegel (yellow shirt and white shirt); and Neil Kantor (black "Egypt" sweatshirt). The pictures are not anything special, but because the lives of their vacation companions are in jeopardy, the people in them have become newsworthy. Frank Hodes already seems like a man in mourning. His wife, Mildred; his sister, Viola; and her husband, Seymour Meskin; his cousin Sylvia Sherman; and his two closest friends, Marilyn and Leon Klinghoffer—Americans with unmistakably Jewish names—were aboard the ship when it was hijacked. If any of the hostages are killed, they are among the most likely candidates. Hodes had given his own film away to another photographer.

By nightfall the scene changes as rumors circulate that at least one American has been killed and that the gunmen are Arabs. So far none of the Arab countries have allowed the terrorists refuge. I check into the Meridian Hotel, not bothering to unpack, as I still don't know where the boat is heading. The *Achille Lauro* had spent the night off the Egyptian coast and some kind of negotiations are underway. I don't want to miss any pictures. The next morning, the driver from *Newsweek*'s Cairo bureau and I pick up our Middle East correspondent, Rod Nordland, from the airport. In Kuwait when the story broke, he'd been having trouble with airline connections. His plane is delayed and I can feel myself getting impatient and irritated. At last Nordland appears, and we are on our way. We still have a two-and-a-half-hour journey to the tip of the Suez Canal, where we will join the hundreds of journalists who are converging on murky Port Said.

Soon after we arrive, Egyptian police take the camerapeople to a location overlooking the sea. I can see the figures of four men paddling a small, unescorted dinghy in the very far distance. We are told they are the hijackers although it's impossible to truly know if it is them or not, and we're too far away, even with a long telephoto lens, to identify faces. If it is them, why are they being allowed to row their way to freedom, waving good-bye? (Later, we'll learn that with Egypt's permission, two mediators from the PLO had in fact persuaded the four heavily armed members of the Palestine Liberation Front who took command of the ship to abandon it in return for safe passage out of the country.)

Apart from some of the local Egyptians, few of us really know where we are and none of us know at which dock the *Achille Lauro* will finally anchor now that the hostage crisis is over. Automatically we herd together, fearing that one of us might get left behind. Every fifteen minutes or so, a new rumor percolates through the port and a blast of footsteps is heard racing down a street with a furious mixture of international obscenities echoing around the harbor. I'm in the pack, running with the mob of crazed cameramen, our feet pounding the pavement from one dock to another. My cameras whip against my ribcage as we stampede to yet another entryway, my camera bag sliding off my shoulder. My eyes sting from sweat. The weight of the crowd crushes me against the iron-mesh gate. And then I feel hands grabbing at me. An Italian cameraman lifts me into the air, tossing me and my cameras aside, so that he can possess my number-one position. Fury and blood gallop through my veins. Nobody says a word. He's stronger and bigger than I am and so is his equipment.

Then another burst of motion as we mass along the edge of the dock, staking out a spot with our tripods and cameras. *Newsweek* has four photographers on assignment, which means that we're competing with each other as well as with everyone else. Ten minutes after we've quieted down, a Reuters photographer who arrived late leaps into the line where *Newsweek* photographer Peter Turnley is standing. Peter goes into a rage, heaving the guy from the row while bashing him on the head with his own cameras.

For the moment, this seems to be the most significant activity. The hostages are nowhere in sight, the drama of the last two days played without principal characters. All we've seen is a long, winding gangplank that leads up to the Italian cruise ship, guarded by a bank of youthful-looking Egyptian police, all of which I frame with a wide-angle lens in the late afternoon light. And once again at sunset. And then at dusk. And during the evening with the ship's lights flinging white lightning-like squiggles upon the darkening sea.

It's cold on the dock. Most of us are hungry. I begin to envy the reporters who have stayed away from this. There's no longer any mystery to the story. By nighttime the entire press corps knows that Leon Klinghoffer, a sixty-nine-year-old American Jew, has been murdered, he and his wheelchair thrown overboard. The one image the press can get for the world to see is of his widow, Marilyn, when she departs from the Italian cruise ship.

Late into the night, U.S. Ambassador Veliotes suddenly arrives with the group of American Jews I'd photographed at the Concorde Hotel. They're whisked past our lenses and onto the gangplank where we're not allowed, surrounded by Egyptian security and American Embassy personnel. Frank Hodes's back is facing our cameras as the press call after him. He glances at us for a split second. "We just had some bad news. I'm too upset to turn around."

We wait. Someone loans me a windbreaker. I long for a bubble bath, room service, a warm, cozy bed, while watching specks of amber from cameramen's cigarettes. Others of us are stretched out on the grimy dock, desperately trying to slumber. And then dawn. I get up and stretch my legs, my body numb from lack of sleep. Everyone's grumpy.

By mid-morning the four of us on assignment for *Newsweek* decide to take turns going to the hotel for a shower and a quick bite to eat. After my turn I come back an hour and fifteen minutes later, only to find that Mrs. Klinghoffer has been escorted from the *Achille Lauro* during my absence. The rest of the day I'm despondent and depressed. Ashamed, actually. I missed the one picture that my foreign editor would expect. How can I explain the void when he looks through my film? Editors don't like to think about a photographer's problems, nor do they care to hear explanations. They tend to measure how good you are by the ratio of assignments to pictures published.

The only thing Mrs. Klinghoffer said as the press swarmed around her was "Get away." She barely looked up, I'm told. I didn't have to be there to know the scene or to realize how I would have behaved. Our conduct is taken for granted, our aggression toward our subjects somehow looked upon as an accomplishment. You get the best images you can whatever the cost. This is our principal purpose, our one and only objective. There are no boundaries, no inhibitions, no ethical considerations. On location we are all carried away by the scent of news and the hunt for the appropriate imagery, regardless of any finer sensitivities we might have as private citizens in the quiet of our off-duty moments.

During my shift, the rest of the hostages finally come into view. They wave to our cameras; the ordeal is over. Some of them walk to a spot on one of the decks to show us where two passengers had been ordered by the gunmen to push Klinghoffer over the railing. We wait until everyone comes off the ship, after which we all head back to Cairo. The story, at least as far as the dusty environs of Port Said, is finished. Our film must now be put on the next plane to New York.

The following afternoon, however, someone tips me off to the time and place of Mrs. Klinghoffer's departure from Egypt. I switch the film in my camera from color slide to color negative so that if I happen onto anything special a print can easily be made and a photograph wired. I slip away to the designated location, where I luck into a series of shots: a smiling Frank Hodes reunited with his wife, Mildred, and his sister, Viola; Marilyn Klinghoffer with her close friends as they're getting ready to leave Cairo. And then, click. I have the image I want: a three-quarter profile of Mrs. Klinghoffer's face looking out of the car window as she departs for the airport. Her shoulders are cloaked in widow's black, her expression is bitter, her eyes full of agony. And it's exclusive. I rush back to the hotel to call Jimmy Colton at *Newsweek*, hoping this might make up for yesterday's mishap. He tells me to wire the photo via AP first thing in the morning.

Paula, AP's photographer in Cairo, says she's too busy with other things. I'm not asking for charity. *Newsweek* will pay AP an exorbitant fee to have my picture, which is called a "special," developed and transmitted. To make the layout for this week's issue, the photograph of Mrs. Klinghoffer must be in Newsweek's office by late morning New York time. I argue and plead with her but she refuses to help, claiming she doesn't have the capability to print color anyway. On my way out of the office, I notice a thick 11 x 14 manila envelope, addressed to AP's headquarters in New York, lying on the unmanned desk at the front entrance. The package is unsealed and looks suspicious. I peek inside when I'm sure no one's watching and discover a stack of color photographs of Mrs. Klinghoffer. Paula just doesn't want to deal with a competitor's pictures since her best photographs are sent to Newsweek also.

I race over to Reuters and explain my dilemma. The darkroom technician develops my film immediately so it can dry and be edited while she finishes transmitting Reuters' pictures. The procedure for wiring color is exactly the same as for black and white, except that the same photograph must be transmitted three times using a different color filter: magenta, cyan, and yellow.

It's now 1:40 p.m. in Cairo before the print has been made. Fortunately with the time difference, we're still seven hours ahead. In order for the image to be received intact, you must have a good phone link, and there's interference on the telephone line, which causes trouble with the transmission. Communications in Cairo are erratic at best. We lose another two hours before the line clears up. By 4 p.m., the picture is on its way to Reuters' head office and editing center in Washington, D.C., where it will be transmitted directly to Newsweek. I telex Jimmy to let him know of its imminent arrival.

For some inexplicable reason, my photograph of Mrs. Klinghoffer is received three hours after the magazine's deadline, having been held up by Reuters in Washington. But the real scoop, according to Jimmy, is that Time, whom we call "Brand X," and Newsweek have both been beaten by "Snooze," the nickname for U.S. News & World Report. Their cover is a pre-hijacking cruise picture that Newsweek had hoped I'd find among the passengers' film: a color photograph of Leon Klinghoffer in his wheelchair on the deck of the Achille Lauro.

16

Caviar, Khat, and Cover Pix

(OCTOBER 1985)

Yasser Arafat, back on the world stage, is casting himself as the savior of the *Achille Lauro*, even suggesting on television that the elderly Leon Kling-hoffer had died of a heart attack.

This time his oratory is not convincing. Klinghoffer's body has washed ashore off the coast of Syria. An autopsy performed in Rome determined he'd died of gunshot wounds, fired at point-blank range. And the press knows that the gunmen who pirated the ship have been identified as members of the Palestine Liberation Front, one of the more radical factions of the PLO, headed by Mohammed Zeidan, better known as Abu Abbas, an Arafat loyalist and close associate. The PLF is believed to have a large number of gunmen in Iraq, Lebanon, and Libya. Their raids are spectacular, daring, and dangerous. In March 1981, the PLF became the first terrorist organization to use motorized hang gliders in an attempt to cross the border and reach Haifa; a month later, it tried to cross the border in a hot-air balloon. Both attempts failed.

Everybody is now looking for Abu Abbas. As the man who mastermind-ed the hijacking of the *Achille Lauro* and who had also been one of the PLO mediators who ended the crisis, he is this week's story. Based in Bagh-dad, he travels on a diplomatic passport supplied by Iraq. Thirty-six years old, he is Palestinian, hotheaded, good-looking, undoubtedly armed to the hilt, and allegedly unpredictable. He's scheduled to be the next *Newsweek* cover.

The problem is that Abbas has vanished. He made his getaway with the four hijackers aboard an Egyptian plane, which was intercepted by Ameri-can fighter jets and forced to land at a U.S. airbase in Sicily. Italian au-thorities arrested the hijackers but permitted Abbas to fly to Rome, where he slipped into an Egypt Air uniform and out of the Leonardo da Vinci Airport, with the Italian government's help, on a flight to Belgrade. Rumor suggests he might be in South Yemen or Iraq, although he last surfaced in Yugoslavia for interviews despite Ronald Reagan's public threat: You can run, but you can't hide.

I decide to fly to the Yemen Arab Republic with *Newsweek*'s correspondent Rod Nordland. We're going there as opposed to anywhere else because we both happen to have visas. The Yemen Arab Republic issued invitations to a group of journalists who wished to cover the anniversary of their revolution, which by chance is occurring this very week. But we're not interested in the festivities.

The idea, Rod tells me, is to get to North Yemen, talk our way across the border into communist South Yemen (for which neither of us have visas) and, if we're successful, hire a car to take us the remaining 170 or so kilometers to the capital, Aden. Once there, we might discover someone who can lead us to Abbas's hideaway and, if he's there, we'll convince him that a *Newsweek* cover story would be good for him. Then I'll have to find a way to get the exclusive pictures to New York before deadline. We have three days.

I envision winding up south of the Saudi Arabian border without a single frame. I'm in the air again, soaring into the night. This is the feeling I love: voyage as steps, leading into other worlds. A gathering of the unknown. A silent, strange waltz of the soul. Dance, Pegasus, dance. Winds whisper under your feet. Already I'm impatient to land.

We touch down near the bottom of the Arabian Peninsula on top of a volcanic plateau. Sana'a, one of the oldest cities in the world, is nearly nine thousand feet above sea level. The city is so surprising that I wonder if I'm suffering from vertigo. Everything around me is the color of ginger and slightly askew, as if the altitude has dislodged the center of each site. The streets are a series of jagged dashes, crooked tracks, layers of mud and sand that spill over into cockeyed slabs of hand-baked mud with swirls of lacy lime wash, decorating the elaborate array of towering gingerbread houses, all of which lean dangerously. It looks as if a bunch of mad minds worked separately on the same city, each one suspicious of the others' modus operandi, neither fully accepting the others' interpretation, yet equally obsessed with making transmutable mythic shapes out of bricks of mud.

We stop at the Ministry of Tourism, where Rod and I collect a variety of travel permits and maps. We'll fly to the southern city of Taiz tomorrow and from there try to cross the border. We hurry back to the fastidious decorum of the Sheraton Hotel to make arrangements. It is almost a quarter past eleven. At noon the entire country shuts down for a four-hour siesta.

Later on, we take a taxi for a brief tour to Sana'a's souk. We get out in the midst of what was once, in pre-Islamic times, one of the seasonal markets for Arabs on the Arabian Peninsula. I feel as if we've ambled into a medieval scene in a low-budget Hollywood movie. The men parade through a tangle of alleys wearing calf-length cloth skirts; ragged brown, oversized suit jackets; plastic sandals; multicolored turbans; and foot-long curved daggers at their waists.

The heat turns the sand into particles of dust that waft into the air, bouncing off the ground into dark Yemeni faces. One side of each face looks terribly swollen, as if everyone in sight had some kind of strange malignant tumor as big as a baseball. I'm slightly drunk with this place. And apparently in good company. Anyone who is stationary has a mound of greenery at his side, which we are told is khat, a leafy, local, chewable high. Judging by the fact that everyone's cheek is puffed out to abnormal proportions, sucking the narcotic leaves seems to be a national male obsession, so much so that nothing of importance is discussed here, let alone resolved, before a lengthy afternoon khat session.

Rod and I buy some jewelry, delicate yet intricately designed silver necklaces, sparkling yellow stones and tiny orange beads linked by silver. And some khat.

In the evening we sit in Rod's room, chewing and chewing. I break off a handful of leaves, roll them into a wad, and munch, trying not to swallow the coarse, acidic foliage. After the visions we've encountered today, I'm not sure I even need to get high. At any rate, the khat doesn't seem to have any effect. We finally spit the stuff out, call room service, and order two plates of Persian caviar.

I go back to my room to try to figure out how I'm going to get photos from Aden to New York by Saturday's deadline. There will be no way to wire photographs from Aden. I pick up my pocket flight guide, sit down at the desk, and start thumbing through the lists of potential airline connections just in case our escapade actually works. You have to be a logistical magician and a seer in this business. As far as I can tell, the film would have to make at least three or four different planes to arrive in New York by Saturday. But no matter how I try to work it out, the timing of the flights is too close for the package to be handled by airfreight without missing at least one of the connections. Not only must photojournalists arrive on the scene of a news event (preferably before it happens), but then we have to make sure our film gets halfway around the world before the deadline. Eventually I give up and go to bed.

The 256-kilometer flight to Taiz takes forty minutes. Then there's a thirty-five-minute trip down a pencil-thin road through sleepy green hills before our driver parks in front of a tumbledown outpost. North Yemen's relations with South Yemen tend to flare into clashes sporadically, and two baby-faced soldiers are now gazing at us, wearing camouflage fatigues and clutching AK-47s, as if they're more prepared for some kind of incursion rather than two Americans who claim they're hiking overland across Arabia. We hand them our passports, our mannerisms nonchalant and courteous. They take turns over each page and hand the passports back to us, shaking their heads.

Rod speaks first, slowly explaining how far we've traveled, as they can see from our passports, all over Arabia, and all we want to do now is cross the border into South Yemen. When that doesn't work I attempt emotional persuasion, talking off the top of my head about our good friends who are waiting for us in Aden. The soldiers speak only a few words of English and our Arabic is equally rudimentary, but when they jibe their machine guns toward Rod it's clear that our idea, however novel, is not feasible without a visa.

By nightfall we're back at Sana'a's Sheraton Hotel. Rod is busy gathering information from stringers and talking on the telex to other *Newsweek* reporters as they piece together a cover story on the unsavory man none of us have met, headlined "Wanted! Hunting the *Achille Lauro*'s Top Terrorist." The only thing I have to show for the story is the telex awaiting us from *Newsweek*'s New York news desk:

ATTN: ROD NORDLAND/SHERATON HOTEL, YEMEN ARAB REPUBLIC

SLUG: ABU ABBAS COVER PIX

ROD: IN THE EVENT THAT THE ABBAS INTERVU COMES OFF AND CAROL SPENCER WILL HAVE FILM TO HANDCARRY TO NY, PHOTO DEPT HAS GONE AHEAD AND ISSUED PREPAID TICKET IN HER NAME IN HOPES THAT SHE'LL BE ABLE TO MAKE THE SCHEDULE:

ADEN TO SANAA VIA YEMEN AIR #405 DEP 7:20 PM ETA 8:10 PM FRIDAY; SANAA TO FRANKFURT VIA YEMEN #740 DEP 1:00 AM ETA 7:25 AM SATURDAY; FRANKFURT TO PARIS VIA LUFTHANSA #110 DEP 8:55 AM ETA 10:AM SAT.; PARIS TO NY VIA AF001 CONCORDE DEP 11:00 AM ETA 8:30 AM SATURDAY. IF SHE CAN DO ALL THAT WITHOUT A HITCH, PHOTO WILL PROBABLY BUY LUNCH ON SATURDAY.

ATTN: FRANCOIS LOCHON
ONE WEEK CHASING DOWN THE ELUSIVE MASTERMIND BEHIND PALES-
TINIAN SEAJACKING. WINDING UP SOUTH OF SAUDI ARABIAN BORDER
WITHOUT SINGLE FRAME. WHAT A LIFE. BE HOME BY LATE TONIGHT AND
SHOULD SEND HUSSEIN PIX TO YOU BY MIDWEEK AIRFREIGHT IF THAT'S
OK. CAN BE REACHED IN DIXIE IF TV INTERESTED IN BIRTHDAY PROFILE.
WARM REGARDS, CAROL.

PART 4

Inside Terror, Inc.

LOCATION/YEAR: JORDAN, THE WEST BANK, CYPRUS, LEBANON;
DECEMBER 1985–MARCH 1986

The ultimate wisdom of the
photographic image is to say:
"There is the surface.
Now think—or rather feel,
intuit—what is beyond it,
what the reality must be like
if it looks this way."
—SUSAN SONTAG

17

Dance into Darkness

(DECEMBER 1985)

Sadness tethers its darkness to the space around me. The type of sadness that swells up, so that for a few minutes I feel startled by an uncomfortable effort to swallow. Denver Airport this morning is overcrowded with post–New Year's travelers carrying the residue of their Christmas celebrations in festive shopping bags. Cross-country and downhill skis, nonchalantly balanced atop athletic shoulders, fill the airport walkways between Rocky Mountain connections. Everybody is either hurrying or waiting.

I cling to my older sister, Ellen, her smooth stomach slightly rounded in the fifth month of pregnancy, her eyes tearing as she presses against me. I'd left Jerusalem to spend the holidays in Aspen with her family, happy to have a break from the Middle East. But there is no escape. Television broadcasts relayed the pandemonium timed to happen simultaneously as seven Palestinian gunmen plucked out American men, women, and children at the TWA, Pan Am, and El Al airport check-in counters in Rome and Vienna. The victims' bodies laid charred and distorted, an autographed testimonial to the frailty of the United States' foreign policy. The next morning the telephone rang. It was Jimmy Colton. "When are you going back?" he asked.

I heave my two duffel bags onto the weighing ramp at Continental Airlines. "But what if something happens to you?" Ellen says as I calmly explain that whenever I'm on assignment, I'm automatically covered by *Newsweek*'s insurance policy.

"Some consolation if you're kidnapped," she snaps.

"Their secretaries probably make more than you do, and they certainly don't have to risk their lives," says my brother-in-law. "What's the value of being a foreign correspondent or a journalist of any sort, for that matter? Especially in the Middle East. And a photographer's really passé. News magazines are a week behind television. Why do you burn yourself out for pictures that have already been aired on TV?"

His questions continue to echo, dissonant variations to my own soul-searching.

A group of teenagers sits nearby in the departure lounge, new recruits into the U.S. Army. They look too young, as if Uncle Sam has mistakenly produced a line of starched green uniforms for boys and then decided to outfit them with fresh faces for promotional purposes. I watch one of them read, from beginning to end, a three-page handwritten letter, over and over. Will I take a picture of him one day, determinedly defending proclaimed American interests somewhere, helpless eyes staring back at me—the latest victim of yet another outrage?

My flight to New York is announced. From New York I'll take another flight to Amman to begin work on my latest assignment: a cover story for *Newsweek* about terrorism. From a news magazine's point of view, the subject sells. It's sexy—"Inside Terror, Inc."—read all about it.

I board the plane, shove my camera bags under the seat in front of me, secure a pillow, fasten my seatbelt, and pretend I'm asleep so I won't have to talk to whoever is seated next to me.

Journalists Are Used to Danger

(JANUARY 1986)

I sit in the lobby of the InterContinental hotel in Amman, waiting for a car and stewing. So far I have nothing to send to New York. How could I? What is there to photograph?

The more I try to visualize a story about terrorism, the more I'm in a quandary about what to photograph. First, there are the theoretical questions. What is terrorism? Who is a terrorist and through whose eyes? What are the implications of the word and the psychology behind its use? Why does terrorism occur? Then the practical questions. Where should I go? What kind of pictures should I take? Who should I, and who should I not, photograph?

"Do whatever you can," Jimmy Colton said when he gave me the assignment to shoot the cover story about Libyan, Syrian, and PLO-sponsored groups that kill in the name of Palestinian rights. "We know it's difficult."

The concierge sidles up to me, jarring me from my thoughts. "A driver is waiting for you," he whispers.

I go outside and get into the car, anxious for my appointment with Abu Jihad and hoping he can help provide a solution to my dilemma on how to illustrate this story. As the car approaches his home, two armed Palestinian bodyguards open the front door and wave aside the Jordanian soldiers standing guard. I'm ushered into the sprawling one-story house without being frisked. Abu Jihad is standing in his living room dressed, as usual, in an expensive, beautiful, deep-charcoal-gray leisure suit and black Gucci shoes.

"Did you hear we have a new baby boy?" he asks.

"No. Congratulations." I put my hand out and he grasps it, a broad smile on his thin lips.

He invites me to sit down on one of the giant velvet-covered sofas, excuses himself, and reemerges carrying a framed 8 x 10 photograph in one hand and a round brass tray of Arabic coffee in the other.

He hands me the black-and-white picture of his latest born, his movements unhurried. "Do you like it?"

"Yes, it's lovely," I say.

"I took it myself," he confesses shyly.

———

Khalil Wazir, for this is his real name, comes across as an ordinary middle-aged man. So ordinary I can't recall first meeting him. I could tell you that I've been to his house in Amman at least half a dozen times for various assignments; that I've sat with him to talk privately on at least as many occasions; that his manner is quiet, polite, coolheaded, low-key. His clothes are always freshly pressed, his brown hair parted neatly off-center on the left, his round face shiny as a polished apple, his mustache meticulous, his dark eyes placid. When I'm with him I think to myself, no, it's just not possible. This man couldn't be military commander of the PLO. He couldn't be the man many consider one of the most legendary terrorists in the Middle East.

And yet there are the two pistols at his hip, the ubiquitous bodyguards, and his mythic reputation as "Abu Jihad," father of the holy war, architect of the armed struggle. In 1975, his fighters landed by boat and stormed a Tel Aviv beachfront hotel in a mission in which eighteen people were killed. There was the coastal hijacking in 1978, when Palestinian commandos infiltrated Israel by sea and captured a crowded bus—thirty-three were killed and eighty-two wounded. Last year, more than twenty Palestinian guerrillas were killed and several captured when the Israelis sunk a ship filled with PLO fighters who were supposed to land on a beach south of Tel Aviv, hijack a bus to the Defense Ministry, and blow up the heavily guarded compound. This too was Abu Jihad's operation. And the fact that Abu Jihad is constantly trying to smuggle weapons and explosives into Palestinian hands in Israel. Yet despite all this, Abu Jihad is an extremely likable guy.

———

"Carol," he says over coffee, "if you really want to understand something about terrorism, you must go to Lebanon. Visit our camps. Go talk to our people. Our fighters."

"Abu Jihad, you know the situation. It's too dangerous. Particularly as a photographer. I'd be too visible."

"Journalists are used to danger."

"I'm not interested in being kidnapped."

"We are ready to help you."

"What do you mean?"

"We'll arrange everything. Don't go to Beirut. Go only to Sidon. Spend some time in Ein el-Hilwe and Miyeh Miyeh. Our fighters control the territory there. We are very strong again, like in '82. You'll have our protection. Think about it. I know you have courage."

———

Ein el-Hilwe, with a population of over thirty thousand, is the largest Palestinian refugee camp in Lebanon. At least another thirty thousand Palestinians reside within the vicinity of Sidon. And I know what Abu Jihad says is true. Arafat's fighters have returned to southern Lebanon, though their numbers have not been disclosed. The whole area has probably the strongest Palestinian concentration in Lebanon and, well known as a training ground for Palestinian fighters, is periodically bombed in Israeli air raids. Miyeh Miyeh, a small camp near Ein el-Hilwe, now seems to be their base, with a military training camp run by the PLO for children between the ages of six and twelve.

Lebanon is tempting. More than that. If I want a cover photograph, it's the only logical place to be. Why shouldn't I take Abu Jihad up on his offer?

———

Abu Jihad and I discuss what I'll be allowed to photograph, the problems surrounding my personal safety, and how to bypass West Beirut. Another man introduced as "K" joins us.

"Why not travel directly to Sidon by boat?" Abu Jihad says. "I think that might be best. We can make the necessary arrangement from Cyprus."

I imagine myself sailing the Mediterranean Sea in a collapsible rubber dinghy, tightly wedged between a crew of armed PLO bodyguards. The image is funny but the reality is not—there are no passenger boats to Sidon. I think of the *Atavarius*, a PLO-owned vessel downed by an Israeli gunboat in the eastern Mediterranean last year. "How would it be possible," I ask him, "and why by boat?"

"It's safer than the airport. K can arrange for you to be a passenger on one of the commercial boats that sail to Sidon. There are quite a few shipping companies that make the trip. And it might be interesting for you."

"How often are these boats stopped by Israeli Navy patrols?"

"Often enough."

"How risky is it?"

"I wouldn't suggest the idea if I thought it was too risky. You're an American journalist. And you'll be under my protection. I don't want you to have any problems."

"Abu Jihad, you must guarantee that there won't be any PLO fighters aboard this boat."

"I know that, Carol."

"And no weapons either."

"I know that too. K will check out everything beforehand. Contact him as soon as you get to Cyprus. He'll be leaving tonight. You are in good hands. By the way, did you know Abu Ammar arrived early this morning?"

"It was rumored."

"He wants to see you."

———

I sit in my hotel room in Amman. In between phone calls and attempts to arrange assorted visas, I ponder Abu Jihad's offer and the dependability of the man himself. Why I should go. Why I shouldn't go.

I'm anxious about how my pictures could be used by *Newsweek*, about how this conflict will be oversimplified. The more I am exposed to the complexities of the Middle East, the more I find the situations turned into media events defying stereotypical photographic representation. I think about the connections between "the story" and the manner in which real people are constructed or contrived in photographs, how images that purport to have captured real life can be used by the mass media to perpetuate a specific way of looking at the world, how the lives of people seen through the camera's lens become a commodity for the international news media. Will the people I photograph die if their faces are used on the cover? Or will they become heroes? The more I question, the more I'm forced to ask myself about the nature of photojournalism, ethical concerns that the business raises and the issue of representation itself.

And then I realize it doesn't matter what the story says, what pictures are used, what facts are created or unraveled, what myths dashed or darned. I know I'm going to Lebanon. I have to.

19

He Who Builds

(JANUARY 1986)

Abu Ammar, meaning "He Who Builds," or "Father Builder," is the nom de guerre of Yasser Arafat, and for over a week I've been trying to catch up with him. Even his closest advisors never know exactly when he will take off or where his magical mystery tour might halt.

It's close to midnight when a driver picks me up at my hotel. Along the highway, he pulls over to the side of the road and turns off the engine. A black Mercedes pulls in behind us. I'm told to change automobiles. Ten minutes later we park in front of a darkened building on the outskirts of Amman. Inside the small entrance hall loom several armed PLO guards. I recognize the one who escorts me in the elevator to the top-floor apartment suite where the acrid smell of nicotine greets me, as do twenty-some pairs of male eyes. I do not see Yasser Arafat, but I know he is here. Someone offers me a seat, then a cigarette, then baklava with a cup of coffee.

Whispering "he wants to see you now," Abu Khaled ushers me through the smoky anteroom into a small sitting room. The "Old Man," as longtime aides like to call Arafat, is sitting in a straight-backed chair, scrutinizing a stack of documents on his lap, the expression on his face utterly concentrated. I stand a few feet in front of him. He looks up at me through a pair of black-rimmed oversized reading glasses.

"What is this *Newsweek* story everyone's talking about?" he asks, laying down his red felt-tip pen.

"It's a special project about terrorism," I reply.

"What does that mean?" he inquires.

"It means it'll be a cover story."

"Is it important?"

"From your point of view? It depends. If the story's straightforward, I mean, if it discusses terrorism in the region, who sponsors it, its history and background, the cycle of mutual retaliation, pinpoints those who are really active, explains how terrorist cells operate, and so on, then yes, I suppose it will be important."

The PLO chief listens to me intently and then asks one question. "Do you think we should cooperate?"

"That's impossible for me to answer. Look, the story's about terrorism. No matter what, you're not going to like what's written. But they're going to talk about you anyway. And the PLO will, in one way or another, be associated with the story. So for that reason alone, yes, I think you should talk."

For a minute or two he's silent. "Okay, tell your reporters that I agree to be interviewed. As will anyone else they wish to speak to."

"Abu Ammar, you do know that I'm only a photographer. I have no control over the content of the story. I don't even have control over how my own pictures will be used, and before I forget, I'll need some new pictures of you."

"I know that, Carol," his voice softens. "By the way, I hear you'll be visiting our camps in Lebanon."

———

It's 1:30 in the morning. I call New York and tell Jimmy Colton I'm going to Lebanon. I have protection, and I'm sure I'll be able to come up with exclusive material. Anyway, I tell him, there's no other way to illustrate this story.

"How much time do you need?" Jimmy asks.

"A few days, I think."

"Okay," he says. Neither of us mention the conversation we'd had over Christmas after the airport attacks, when it was decided that under no circumstances would an American photographer be sent to Lebanon. We both know a cover story is at stake. But this is my choice. He hasn't asked me to go.

"I have to pick up a few things in Jerusalem," I say. "I'll call you from Cyprus on Sunday."

20

Private Conversations (II)

(JANUARY 1986)

Before going back to Jerusalem, my good friend Sana Alul, a Palestinian journalist known for her close ties to the PLO, introduces me to her brother Hamdullah. In May 1985, he, along with 1,150 Palestinians held in prisons throughout the occupied territories, was released in exchange for six Israelis who were captured in Lebanon and held by Ahmed Jabril's Popular Front for the Liberation of Palestine–General Command. The Palestinians were subsequently deported to Amman.

Hamdullah is thirty-one and, like Sana, tall and handsome, but a bit gaunt, as one might expect after thirteen years in prison. Clad in blue jeans and a denim shirt, he has a gentle voice, a gentle way of being. He is subdued and intense. I sit down with him, hoping to learn more about terrorism and its perpetrators. I turn on my tape recorder, and he tells me his story.

"I am from Nablus in the West Bank. Legally, I cannot ever go back. When I was released in the exchange of prisoners in 1985, a great wave of unrest followed. We are still wanted by the Israelis.

"I joined the PLO in 1972. I was a student, seventeen years old, and had lived all my life in the shadows of the Israelis and their footsteps. We Palestinians knew that the Revolution was our only way to find ourselves and preserve our self-pride. So, after becoming a member of the PLO, I acquired the necessary training and worked with an armed group inside Occupied Palestine.

"Our situation was very difficult, our people scattered in refugee camps in Jordan, Syria, Lebanon, as well as in the Occupied West Bank and Gaza

Strip. This is still the situation today. We know all that. Just as the Israelis know deep down inside that we have the right to strive and fight for our homeland.

"I was given the assignment to plant bombs in a location where there were military people as a reaction to the Israelis confiscating Arab land and property and building up settlements inside Occupied Palestine. The basis of our Revolution is the Armed Struggle. Our struggle is a struggle to survive. Have you ever heard of a country being occupied and its children doing nothing to get it back? After that I was captured and sentenced to life imprisonment.

"Of course it was clear that when people did military operations inside Israel they would be captured and sentenced for long years. But if there was an operation, the Israelis did not just arrest the one who did it. They detained maybe one hundred persons. I was arrested and interrogated many times long before I joined the Revolution. Hundreds of innocent people were imprisoned and sentenced to long years in prison just because they were members of the PLO. That in itself was a reason for me to join the PLO.

"After being captured, I was moved to Ashkelon prison and put in a section known as the X's, where the prisoner is not only interrogated but also taught the rules of the prison: how to fold up the bed cover, how to answer the jailer, how to speak, when to speak, and with whom. It consisted of thirty cells with very hard living conditions. I was forced to take off all of my clothes in front of ten or twelve jailers, and as soon as I was stark naked I was beaten severely and endlessly. I had to answer their questions using the word 'Sir,' and when I didn't I was beaten again. The faster a prisoner accepted and learned the rules, the quicker he could leave the X's section.

"There were around six hundred prisoners in Ashkelon. Rooms were overcrowded, seventeen people to a cell with the windows barred closed. We were allowed out of our rooms for only twenty minutes a day. We went outside in pairs, with our hands cuffed behind our backs, and we were not allowed to talk. Whoever broke the rules was given two–three days in solitary confinement and five days of bread and water only. A doctor visited the prison once every two weeks. We were not given proper medical care. Aspirin was handed out for all kinds of illness. Guerrillas injured in operations did not have their wounds taken care of.

"The prisoners started a revolution inside the prison's walls. We organized ourselves secretly. We were not allowed paper, so our thoughts and ideas were written down on the packages of butter and sent by hand from one room to another. In addition, we began a hunger strike. Imagine six hundred weak, humiliated, and beaten prisoners starting a hunger strike to achieve such small human rights as to stop saying 'Sir' to our jailers and to have sufficient medical care. Even injured and badly hurt prisoners insisted on joining our strike.

"The Israeli police minister, who had once said we Palestinians do not deserve to live, came to our prison to discuss ways of ending the strike. The word 'Sir' was abolished and the beatings stopped. We then realized that nothing could be achieved inside the prison walls unless we continued struggling for the most simple, basic human rights.

"We divided ourselves into committees that were responsible for every aspect of our lives. Education. Administration. Politics. News. The first decision taken by the committees was to eliminate illiteracy. All six hundred prisoners must learn how to read and write and become literate. We did not have any pens or any paper. We picked up small chalk stones from the grounds outside, hid them in our clothes, and the floors in our rooms were used as 'blackboards.' The program to end the ignorance of all the prisoners was of a six-month period, and it was a success.

"By then, we were so well organized that the strongest military force in the world could not stop us. Each and every one of us had something to do. During the day we would teach and read, and every night there was a meeting. For instance, Saturday nights were for political discussions. Sunday nights we held educational seminars. On Monday nights, there was a court session, where we would judge Carter, Sadat, and others. It was a way to see everyone's point of view and to talk about other world issues. We also discussed international news, such as the Vietnam War, Nicaragua, the Soviet Union, and made contact with other prisoners in other prisons. All prisons interacted as one whole unit. We would write a note and make it into a tiny ball, transferring it to the outside mouth-to-mouth when kissing visiting relatives. What happened in one prison was quickly followed in all prisons.

"Israeli authorities tried hard to stop us. They isolated Palestinian leaders and the heads of the committees and imposed punishment on all prisoners. They tried to suppress and abort the detainees' nationalism and patriotic feelings, but by then we knew we could not and should not stop. The prison had become our university, and the Israelis finally gave up and permitted us to meet every night. We achieved many things, like to have writing tools.

"We learned Hebrew by stealing Hebrew newspapers from the rubbish. We translated news that was important for the Revolution and produced our own newspaper inside the prison. This was forbidden of course, but the

Palestinian fighter is very good in hiding forbidden things. In my prison we had sixty transistor radios and those were at the top of the forbidden list, yet only one or two were discovered.

"The radios were more precious to us than gold. One of the committees, made up of about twelve prisoners, was responsible for picking up news from all over the world. This committee worked at night listening to the radio from Monte Carlo and London and every morning would publish a bulletin of world news. The news, and even copies of books, were transferred from one prison to another by prisoners who were themselves transferred to other prisons, or with visiting family members. This was top secret.

"Later, the Red Cross was permitted to distribute books to our prison. These books—religious stories, Arab literature, and some novels—circulated and everybody read them. Most of the prisoners knew them by heart. Later, we made a kind of deal with the Red Cross to bring us the books we wanted to read—about Castro, Che Guevara, and Régis Debray, for instance—after changing their covers because political and revolutionary books were not allowed. Our families would often help by getting the books, replacing their covers, and then dropping them off with the Red Cross who would, of course, give them to us.

"In 1976, we began to plunge into a new stage of struggle in Ashkelon prison and informed our families, the Red Cross, and other organizations that we were preparing for another hunger strike. Our demands were improvement of health and sanitary conditions; mattresses to sleep on and decent covers; proper medication; decent food and to be allowed to cook our own meals; more books; to go out in the sun for longer periods of time; and the removal of iron from the windows of our rooms.

"During the first nine days of the hunger strike we ate nothing, but we drank large quantities of water. On the tenth day, jailers were brought in to us disguised as doctors. They didn't know anything about medication. They were guards. They took us one by one to what was called a medication room, where they would ask us if we would stop the strike. If we refused, they forced a tube into our nose and down our stomach and poured 70 mg of milk into it. The tube was inserted so harshly that when they took it out, it was usually full of blood. This procedure was done every day until the end of the strike.

"For forty-five days, five hundred Palestinians refused to take meals. We could not believe it. We thought the hunger strike would last for fifteen to twenty-five days, but forty-five days surpassed all expectations. Every night a message of support circulated among all the prisoners to give us strength and support. The message was 'we are who we are.'

"The tubes were used every day. On the twenty-second day of the strike, the authorities decided to isolate us. They divided us into three groups and sent us to three different places: Jalame in the north, Abu Kabir, and Kfar Yona, where I was taken.

"On the forty-fifth day, a committee from the Knesset met with the leaders of the hunger strike and discussed and approved most of our demands, but the prison authorities did not abide by this agreement. We began preparing ourselves for a new strike because we were not given what had been promised.

"So, forty-five days after the end of the first hunger strike, a new hunger strike began. Messages of support poured in for the hunger strikers. Mothers of prisoners met in the Red Cross and joined their sons in their hunger strike. The United Nations met to discuss our strike. The world knew about us. This made us feel like we were taking part in our Revolution in our own way.

"We stopped on the twentieth day when all our demands were approved and implemented. Conditions began to get better. Israelis tried their best to treat us humanely. They even allowed us two hours outside our rooms instead of twenty minutes. The conditions in prisons improved considerably, but there were still cases of ill treatment.

"We realized that each one of us has a purpose in life. We made contact with all the Palestinian organizations, student unions, youth groups, and women's unions to teach what we learned inside the prison to our people outside. When any one of us was released, he would go where he thought he was needed. For instance, if there was a man in prison whose family had a field which no one was caring for, he would organize volunteers to help with the field.

"The authorities began to understand that the prisons were creating leaders in Palestinian society. They brought in a Professor Wertheimer, from Bar Ilan University, who was put in charge of the prisons and established a committee of seven colonels to discuss the situation. He founded a new prison in the desert, which is now called Nafha. He isolated people according to their power inside the prisons.

"In 1980, they began a new strike, which was started in Nafha. After a week, the other prisons, Beersheva and Ashkelon, joined in the strike. The strike was organized between these three prisons. On the ninth day, doctors were sent to Nafha from Siroka Hospital. They had to find the weakest people. They took twenty-six prisoners from Nafha and sent them to Beit Ma'atsar, a new prison near Ramle. These twenty-six were beaten by the guards very badly, and they used the tubes in a hard way. They did not put milk in them. Instead they put water and salt. On the ninth day in Beit Ma'atsar, three prisoners died. It was not accidental.

"The prisoners received support from their relatives and organizations outside, even among some Israelis. The strike continued for thirty-three days. This made Nafha prison just like the other prisons.

"The authorities realized now they could not face the prisoners' power, so they began to deal with them in another way. Now the interior situation among the prisoners is much better. This doesn't mean that there is not torturing still. Once myself and thirty prisoners were sent to our cells for three months a first time and five months a second time.

"Wertheimer himself, when they would make an interview with him on TV or in the newspaper, couldn't deny the organization of the Palestinians inside. He said once he hoped the Israeli prisoners could be like the Palestinian prisoners. Once Wertheimer wrote that he saw the Palestinians late at night sitting around talking about very sensitive things, like Nicaragua, or the Soviet Union, very important issues. He also wrote that the Palestinian prisoners knew about the Israeli situation and society more than the Israelis themselves. They knew about the political parties, the Knesset.

"Another man, responsible for security in the prisons, once said in an interview that he wanted to ask for more money for the prisons in order to bring in guards who were from universities. He was asked why. Because there was an educational gap between the prisoners and the guards, he said. Now they don't allow the guards to speak to the prisoners, because any prisoner could give a guard his point of view.

"We are still fighting for our lands but things are improving. The world has a better view of who we really are politically. Our morale is better than several years ago, and we are trying hard to unify our forces. The Israelis did not think or anticipate that the Revolution would continue after 1967. They thought the guerrilla attacks would end. There is always the possibility of peace, but 80 percent of the Israeli people do not believe we have the right to exist or that we have the right to self-determination. We are convinced that our enemy will not give up a speck of land by negotiations. We call for peace but not the kind of peace that is enforced on us by Israelis. Armed fighting will not stop now. We gain strength from confrontation and fighting. We are not giving up our lands and our homes and especially not our identity. Our situation is very difficult, our forces are scattered. But as long as there are Palestinian children who know and are taught of the Palestinian cause, the Revolution will continue!"

21

Promise Me I Won't Be Touched

(JANUARY 1986)

PRO SPENCER

FROM NEWSWEEK BUREAU BEIRUT

RE: DANGER OF BOAT TRIP

AS YOU PROB AWARE, THERE HAVE BEEN QUITE A FEW INCIDENTS OF
PLO GUYS ARRESTED OR KILLED BY ISRAELI NAVY AS THEY TRY TO SAIL
FROM CYPRUS TO SIDON. YOU SHOULD KNOW THE DANGER MAY BE MORE
CONSIDERABLE THAN COMING IN VIA AIRPORT. IT IS LIKELY YOU'LL BE
STOPPED BY THE ISRAELIS. JUST BE SURE YOU HAVE ALL THE NECESSARY
I.D. TO PROVE YOU ARE AMERICAN AND A PHOTOG WORKING FOR NEWS-
WEEK. SO LONG AS THERE ARE NO ARMED MEN ON BOARD, THERE IS NO
REASON YOU SHOULD HAVE PROBLEMS. BUT IT IS RISKY, AND THE FINAL
DECISION WILL OF COURSE HAVE TO BE YOURS.

In Cyprus, I run off to the hotel bar to talk over my plans with a journalist
friend who knows Lebanon far better than I do.

"You're crazy to even think about it," he says.

"Well, so far they haven't come up with a boat for me."

"The whole idea is ridiculous. Does New York understand what you're
about to do? What if something happens?"

"Yeah, I can just imagine the story. 'An Israeli Navy vessel intercepted
a yacht off the coast of Cyprus today, capturing eleven members of Force
17. An American woman accompanying the terrorists claims she's a photographer working for *Newsweek* magazine. She's being held for further
interrogation.'"

"Look, if you're really bent on going, then tell *Newsweek* to send someone with you. Nobody goes to Lebanon alone."

"I'll have bodyguards."

"From the PLO? They can't even protect themselves. How are they go-ing to protect you? The camps are surrounded by Shiite militiamen."

"That's in Beirut, not Sidon. Anyway, Mehdi will be with me."

"*Newsweek's* driver? Well, that's some consolation. He's a good man. But I still think it's too risky."

"I'm female, remember. They haven't nabbed any women. At least I don't think so."

"Does anyone have your passport information?"

"My editor."

"Give it to me, too. If your office is anything like mine, they've probably misplaced it already. And phone me before you leave."

———

I peel off two tiny yellow Israeli airport security stickers stuck on the side of my suitcase and camera bags, remove the Tel Aviv–Larnaca flight identification tags, and dump my clothing on the bed of my hotel room in Cyprus, methodically checking each and every item for Israeli cleaning tags and pieces of crumpled paper that could prove incriminating. Next, I inspect my camera bags, taking out various receipts written in Hebrew, a pocket-sized Israeli-made memo pad, and some loose change. Finally, I go through my wallet, removing the foreign press card issued by the Israeli government, more receipts, a Jerusalem health club identity card, and the Israeli shekels and coins.

I put these in the manila envelope I brought with me, along with the passport that I use to travel to Israel and my Larnaca–Tel Aviv return airline ticket, seal the envelope, and deposit it in the hotel's safe box, telling the manager I'll pick it up when I return from Lebanon.

———

For hours we sit together over coffee: K and two Palestinian cohorts who belong to what Israelis call a "hostile terrorist organization"; Amnon, an Israeli writer and fifth-generation citizen of what Arabs call the "Zionist entity"; Samir, an Israeli Arab poet plunged into a quagmire of conflict-ing loyalties; and myself, an American Jewish photojournalist who covers the Arab beat. The contradictions of history are disputed then abandoned, battle slogans crumble, and the complexities of political compromise yield to the elasticity of the human heart.

I retell an incident told to a few journalists and myself over breakfast by "W," a U.S. State Department official who specializes in behind-the-scenes Arab-Israeli mediation. At the time, we were all staying at the InterConti-nental Hotel in Jordan, as was Abu Iyad, the PLO's head of intelligence. W had walked out into the lobby from the elevator just as Abu Iyad entered the hotel from the front door. Officially—that is, according to State Department policy—W was not allowed to talk to members of the PLO. So he hid himself in the lobby behind one of the support columns because he was terrified that one of the television cameras might find a way of filming him and Abu Iyad together. We all laughed, understanding the tragic irony of Middle Eastern politics, where warring parties save face by stubbornly refusing to acknowledge each other's presence and the politics of procedure cause a necessary suspension of substance.

———

Later, K meets me in the hotel lobby. He says he's found a boat, but he wants me to go talk to the owner to be sure I'm comfortable with the arrangements.

"He's waiting for you." K hands me the address on a crumpled slip of paper. "This is your contact in Sidon." He gives me an empty matchbook with a telephone number scribbled inside. "His name is Abu Mahmoud. Whatever you do, don't write his name down."

"That's it?" I ask, staring at the number.

"That's all you need. He knows Abu Jihad has sent you. Phone him as soon as you arrive. He will take good care of you."

I walk to the storefront address K has given me, oblivious to my surroundings. The man behind the fish counter looks me over with greedy eyes, then holds out his right hand. "They didn't tell me it was a woman," he says. "Someone else going with you?"

"No, it's just me."

"Could be a problem, you know."

"How come?"

"Well, you're a journalist, right? I'm sure you know the harbor's crawling with Mossad agents, and they know exactly who's aboard what boats. You might look suspicious."

"What do you mean?"

"Just that we have to be careful. Our commercial ships have all-male crews. I don't want any problems."

"Neither do I. Is it possible to go or not?"

"Well, I suppose we can put you down as the cook."

"That's fine. When does your boat leave?"

"Tomorrow, or the day after. Depends on weather conditions. Hope you have a strong stomach. The seas are pretty rough this time of year. There might be a storm coming in. If it does, we'll wait it out."

"How long does the trip take?"

"About eighteen hours. That's if the boat's not stopped by an Israeli patrol."

"And if it is?"

"A delay, for maybe a couple of hours. It depends on whether they decide to inspect the boat or not. Now when you get into Sidon, you know you can't get off right away."

"Why not?"

"The boat's got to go through customs first."

"How long does that take?"

"Most of the day, usually. Depends what time we get in and how many boats are ahead of us. If the port's busy, or if we get in late, you may have to dock overnight in the harbor."

"I see. . . . You're the owner of this boat, right?"

"Yes."

"I want your guarantee on something."

"What?"

"I want you to guarantee that I won't be touched."

"Lady, you're going to be out on the high seas. Just you and a crew of men. I have no control over what may happen."

I walk straight into the telex room at the hotel and begin typing.

ATTN: NEWSWEEK BUREAU BEIRUT/URGENT

WILL NOT BE TAKING BOAT TO SIDON AFTER ALL. REPEAT. HAVE CAN-
CELED BOAT TRIP. INSTEAD WILL ARRIVE BEIRUT AIRPORT ON MEA
FLIGHT TOMORROW MORNING 9:40 A.M. PLS HAVE MEHDI MEET ME.
RGDS, SPENCER

At five in the afternoon, 10 a.m. New York time, I dial my editor.

"Are you sure that's what you want to do?" Jimmy says.

"Yes, I spoke to the Beirut bureau, and they said the airport road's pretty good right now."

"Okay, but we don't want you going into West Beirut."

"It won't be necessary. Mehdi will pick me up, and we'll drive straight to Sidon. I don't want to waste any more time. By the way, I am covered by *Newsweek's* insurance policy, right?" In twelve years of working, this is the first time I've ever asked.

"Yes, both our regular policy and our war insurance."

"You realize I'll be charging danger pay?"

"Yes, we know that. Now keep your head down, and don't take unnecessary risks."

I call K to tell him my plans have changed.

"Your contact is waiting for you," he assures me. "You have nothing to worry about."

But I am worried. I'm putting my life in the hands of the PLO, when all they've given me is a telephone number scrawled inside a matchbook. Can I trust them? I'm working on a story that will probably betray those I've befriended — using their help to do it. Will they be there for me?

———

It's close to midnight — 5 p.m. New York time. I go outside and stand on the edge of my balcony overlooking the night-lit marina. The breeze coming in from the Mediterranean is dry and prickly, the scent of jasmine wafting about. I stand here for a long time and listen to the wind, the way Jim the fisherman, an old family friend, taught me when I was six.

"To observe how the wind blows across the water and from which direction the fish swim," he said, "you must be willing to close your eyes and listen. When you open your eyelids, you will see the swirl of movement with your instinct."

Jim told me that everyone has two voices: one that comes gusting from the mouth without too much thinking, and another that flows like a current into the heart. At home it was often said that I was stubborn, but Jim said my silence had something to do with the inner voice. I needed to hear it, so I never talked much. Some people are born that way. Some need to talk aloud, others need quiet to hear their voice.

It's silent everywhere now. No one is about. For years I've associated silence with safety, finding voice through the reflex of a lens. When I hold a camera to my eyes, the barriers between myself and the world momentarily fade. When Jim and I went fishing beside the canal I felt secure, the same kind of calm I feel in the darkroom.

I go back in my room, but I can't sleep. I pick up the phone to call Jimmy, to tell him this is nonsense. I'm not a war photographer. Who am I kidding? But before dialing I hang up and light a cigarette, eyes on the amber ash. Why are you going, I ask myself: To make a living? For professional credibility? To prove you're courageous? Because you're a woman?

I stare at myself in a travel-worn mirror. An unsettled, obstinate woman engaged in a rootless trek. A gypsy, with not much more than some carry-on luggage to call her own. What price will I pay for my sack full of pictures that recall enormous moments of madness like souvenirs or religious icons?

I tell myself I don't have to go, knowing by tomorrow morning, I'll be there.

22

Lebanon

(JANUARY 1986)

ATTN: ROD NORDLAND/NEWSWEEK CAIRO BUREAU
ROD: NEED TO KNOW CURRENT DEADLINE ON STORY. CAN BE REACHED
IN BEIRUT. RGDS, CAROL.

PRO SPENCER FROM NORDLAND
CAROL: I DON'T THINK MUCH OF YOU STAYING THERE A WEEK. THINK THE
RISKS OUTWEIGH WHATEVER POSSIBLE GAIN, UNLESS YOU HAVE SOME-
THING HOT. IF NOT, I MOST STRENUOUSLY OBJECT. DEADLINE IS END OF
NEXT WEEK. WHEN DO YOU PLAN TO LEAVE BEIRUT?

PRO NORDLAND FROM SPENCER
PLAN TO LEAVE TOMORROW OR WEDNESDAY AT LATEST. AM NOT FOOL-
HARDY. AT LEAST I DON'T THINK SO.

PRO SPENCER FROM NORDLAND
NOBODY IS FOOLHARDY UNTIL THEY GET KIDNAPPED. CALL ME WHEN
YOU ARE OUT.

I spend the day in Shatila refugee camp on the southern outskirts of Beirut.
There, I go with some Palestinian fighters to their barracks. Tiers of sandbags are stacked behind me, just inside the entrance. I stand motionless,
holding a tripod across my body. My camera bag is on the floor by my feet.
All around there are army cots, weapons, and ammunition. I look at the
bullet-marred walls, thinking about the camp's history. Seven or eight fighters walk about—PLO guys, most of them teenagers. On a table in the far
corner is a gray metal box with wires hanging off it. I guess that it is a short-

wave operations radio. Next to it is a hand-carved wooden bench, and next to that an old armoire with ivory inlaid doors. On one of the glass-enclosed shelves, I can see a pair of bongos and a flute.

It's late afternoon and a warm, lemony sunlight crisscrosses the room from two windows. I set up my tripod. Swivel the camera into place. I'm working now, concentrating as I take extraneous wide shots that capture the surroundings. Drawn into their world, and mine, while I recreate its appearance.

Fighter leaning on sandbags. Snap. Fighter at window. Click. Fighter sitting alone, rifle lying across his knees. Fighters posing, PLO flag in background. But I know all along that I want those two, sitting next to each other on the bed near the window, their Kalashnikovs hanging like artwork on the wall behind them. I switch the lens on my camera and reframe the image. Click. Then stand at my tripod waiting, waiting until they forget about me and my camera.

In the photograph they are sheltered for the moment, physically cut off from the action. Yet their feelings, the emotional uncertainty of their lives, confront me immediately. The image mixes innocence with blood and death, puts them in opposition to each other. That flinty look in their eyes tells me, like their camouflaged fatigues, about their struggle to survive, how they've been sucked into their own wearying history, though the soft, almost tender teenage faces insist on their vulnerability.

But the tension in the photograph—their youth versus a war in which their lives are inescapably entangled—is held together in the motion of the fighter on the left, the way he extends one arm above the bed, his hand jutting into the air, his fist tightly clenched. It is the wistfulness of this one unconscious gesture, seen against the guns dangling over their heads, that holds their stark reality in place. Everything is framed around this polarity.

———

I'm taken to another camp, one of the training facilities for children under the age of twelve. I set up my tripod again while the children glance shyly at me. Their instructors issue orders and the children drill, marching back and forth in their green uniforms, pictures of martyred loved ones hanging from their necks, Kalashnikovs at their sides. At first they are stiff, aware of this stranger among them taking pictures. Two young boys run and crouch, bobbing up and down, pointing shoulder-held missile launchers to the sky. Click. An instructor, his arm wrapped around a boy's shoulder, shows him how to use a rifle as if teaching him how to bait a hook.

Click. Two older boys practice hand-to-hand combat with knives. Click. A girl lies flat on her stomach, her head wrapped in white, aiming her rifle at an imaginary foe. Snap. As I work they gradually loosen up, cavorting now for me and my camera. Yet underneath, the expressions on their faces are serious, almost grim. I fold my tripod up and pack my camera bag. I have the photos I want.

PART 5

Travels in Sudan

LOCATION/YEAR: THE SUDAN;
MARCH 1986–APRIL 1986

And we, spectators always,
everywhere, looking at, never
out of everything! It fills us.
We arrange it. It decays.
We rearrange it,
and decay ourselves.

—RAINER MARIA RILKE

23

Sorry, All Lines Are Jammed

(MARCH 1986)

Sudan Airways is overbooked. Hundreds of tall, lean men, all of whom hold a ticket in their hands, pack the terminal, which is strewn with luggage. I guess them to be Sudanese laborers who, having done a stretch of work in Egypt, are returning home before Ramadan, the month of holy fasting when, from dawn until sunset, Muslims are prohibited from eating, drinking, and smoking, and throughout the Arab world business grinds down from its sluggish pace to a ponderous standstill.

I zigzag my way across the lounge, trying not to trip over the clumps of suitcases, all of which seem to be strapped together with yards of string and strips of masking tape. Everyone is wearing thick, loosely fitted turbans and ankle-length jalabiyas cut from white Sudanese cotton that is now creased and dirty as if they have been camped out at Cairo airport for days which, as I think about it, they most probably have. The flight to Khartoum scheduled for last night had failed to materialize. Nor has the one for which we are all now waiting yet landed.

Compulsively, I ask another passenger if he thinks the plane will take off tonight. He shrugs his shoulders. Flights from Cairo to Khartoum are so unreliable they are not even listed on the airport's arrival and departure information roster. Sudan Airways, like Sudan itself, functions on what Arab friends call the IBM system: Insha'allah (if God wills it), Bokra (tomorrow), and Malesh (it doesn't really matter).

After two years in the Middle East I've learned to take things in stride, except the creeping paranoia that occurs while hanging out in terminals most likely to become a target for hijackers. Tense and uncomfortable, I begin plotting escape routes in case gunmen open fire. I see myself standing among the crowd of white Arab robes. If all hell breaks loose, I am the only foreigner and the only woman. It is impossible to push this thought aside. I plop down in a corner with hardly any room to move and sit there for most of the night. In a crunch, I could dive beneath the lanky bodies of my fellow travelers. At least I'm happy to be getting away from the Arab-Jewish conflict, to work on a project that isn't connected, even tangentially, to the emotions of Israelis and Palestinians.

We board at 2:50 a.m. The plane climbs lazily into black space when the clatter begins. Cigarettes are lit from seat to seat across the aisles, everyone chattering wildly. I slump into silence, wanting desperately to sleep. "Malesh," I say to myself, at least we are off the ground. I never have understood why airliners traversing Arab capitals inevitably leave in the dead of night, for flights that generally average only two and a half hours. I decide to order a drink, but alcohol, the steward whispers, is "Mamnoor" (not allowed). Coffee in hand, I realize I'd forgotten that Sharia, the Islamic code of law, governs the conduct of all travelers to the Sudan. For a while I try to decipher the loud and intense conversation around me. The cabin is littered with banana peels, orange peels, mango pits, and ash. I look for a cigarette and light up with everybody else.

By the time we empty out of the plane, my body is numb with exhaustion, brain on automatic. Or perhaps it is the other way around. I'm brain dead and my body is like a machine, sleepwalking through passport control, gradually collecting my bags, which are shoved slowly into a dim hall lacking electricity and porters. Tugging them outside, I stagger toward the one available taxi, reminding myself that the comic routine that now lies in store is thankfully the last ritual.

"How much?" I smile wanly.

"You pay?" It is more an exclamation than a question as the driver's eyes look past my head, sliding from left to right, as if it is inconceivable that he could have lucked into a Western woman who has arrived in Sudan alone.

"Yes. How much to the Hilton Hotel?"

"How much you like?"

"Yalla." (Let's go.) I give up and get in, too tired to haggle.

Dawn in Khartoum. Submachine guns at spooky angles, pointing out from corners of the city's broad avenues, where the shadows of lone soldiers in green battle fatigues slumped against colonial-style buildings form patterns along the sidewalks. The capital at the break of day, barely awake, is drenched in a sallow, grainy light. Street urchins, barefoot and bare-bottomed, dawdle in the dust, along with mangy cats and mongrel dogs, disfigured and all bones. Somewhere nearby, the ash-gray waters of the Blue

Nile blend with the somber brown waters of the White Nile, or maybe it is the other way around. I'm not sure. The wail of an imam hangs into the air and settles evenly, his voice the only sound, as if everywhere.

―――――

It is now 7:40 a.m., twenty-six hours since I slept at all. Over breakfast, in a feeble attempt to orient myself, I look through the tourist brochure that I found in my room while unpacking.

Sudan is the largest country in Africa, roughly the size of Western Europe. The nation's population is as diverse as its wildlife. Sudan's 20 million people belong to an array of different ethnic groups who speak more than one hundred languages and, at last count, were registered in over forty-seven political parties that range from pro-Moscow communists, to pro-Libyan anarchists, to pro-Muslim Brotherhood fundamentalists, to pro-Egyptian Unionists, to rival pro-Iraqi and pro-Syrian wings of the Baath Socialist Party.

While the brochure assured me that the country had "made giant steps toward progress in the last few years under the dynamic leadership of President Jaafar Nimeiri," the economy was bankrupt and the pro-American President Nimeiri had been deposed in a military coup a year ago. The new transitional government restored diplomatic relations with Libya, and known Libyan and Palestinian "terrorists" were turning up on the streets of Khartoum. Americans had been warned by the U.S. State Department to stay clear of the Sudanese capital.

The map of the Sudan shows a handful of towns, an ornate orange-colored mosque that catches the eye, a purple-thin squiggle that depicts the Nile rivers, and a road system that appears to be nonexistent. Wildlife, however, is apparently abundant. Antelope leap without perspective across a stretch of stark desert; a lion paces up and down the border of Uganda; pelicans stand motionless in a pool of water; giraffes flee in the direction of Ethiopia; and in southern Sudan, not far from Zaire, a pair of zebras roam in flat savanna. At the center of the map, near the bank of the White Nile, a tribesman wearing a skirt of elephant grass whirls his spear while camels rest undaunted beneath the shade of a stout baobab tree. Farther down the river, a wild elephant with glittery white tusks thunders after an unsightly black rhino.

I read the information provided, still trying to get a fix on what is where. In eastern Sudan at the Dinder National Park, the tourist brochure tells me "there are lions, giraffes, leopards, kudus, bushbuck, and antelope together with several species of birds such as guinea fowl, vultures, pelicans, storks, king-fishers, and the beautiful crowned cranes." But the outskirts of the park, according to the United Nations, are overcrowded camps with more than 400,000 refugees from Ethiopia.

The southern region, the tourist brochure says, "is characterized by green forests, open parkland, waterfalls, and treeless swamps abounding with birds and wild animals such as elephants, black and white rhinoceros, bongo, common eland, Nile lechwe, lesser kudu, oryx bisa, zebra, crocodiles, hippopotamus, hyenas, buffalo, and the almost extinct shoebill." However, the south is also plagued by 250,000 refugees from Uganda and a vicious civil war. For reasons of safety, the Sudanese government generally won't permit anyone but relief workers to travel there.

In western Sudan, the brochure continues, "there are places of outstanding scenic beauty like Erkowit and Jebel Marra, two famous holiday mountain resorts." There are also 123,000 displaced refugees from Chad.

If the map delights in lively sketches of wildlife, it casually hides the country's darker side. I had come to the Sudan to photograph a cover story for *Newsweek* about third-world diseases. The colorful drawings lure the traveler with primitive tales of African adventure and legendary stories of exotic animal safaris but fail to disclose how one simply gets around. I study the map again, wondering by what routes a person can journey overland.

———

Before arriving here, a rare surge of pragmatic panic inspired a whirlwind visit to a Cairo health clinic, during which my arms, still hopelessly bruised and utterly sore, had been subject to: a needle against yellow fever, which is obligatory if one hopes to go to any other country after having been to the Sudan; a shot of gamma globulin to reduce the risk of infectious hepatitis; and an injection against cholera, which is rumored (though officially denied by Sudanese health authorities) to be endemic. This was followed by a trip to the pharmacy for a coffer full of chloroquine that would hopefully defend me from malaria-bearing mosquitoes; a large dose of antibiotics; and enough anti-diarrhea pills to mess up my system for the next few months. None of this, however, would necessarily shelter me from the perils of a nation whose vast reservoir of medical disorders are supposed to include every species of plague, pest, and parasite imaginable.

I gulp down another cup of coffee, change some dollars into pounds, and wander over to the headquarters of the United Nations Children's Fund (UNICEF), hoping that someone there will give me a decent briefing.

Stephano Di Mistura, coordinator of UNICEF's immunization campaign, greets me with a rueful grin. "Well, you've certainly come to the right place. How much time do you have?" he asks, as I follow him into his office.

"Whatever time you can give me."

"No, I mean how much time are you planning to spend in Sudan?"

"I think the story's due next week, but I'll have to check."

He stares at me in disbelief, then opens one of his drawers and pulls out a map. This one divides Sudan into seven regions and pinpoints major towns. A green line delineates a fairly extensive railway, and here and there I see red dashes, which, according to the index, represent about twelve hundred kilometers worth of sporadic tarmac.

"I guess you've never been here before," he says, "which I suppose isn't all that surprising."

"What do you mean?"

"Sudan's not exactly one of the media's favorite watering holes." He casually begins to list a lexicon of horrors, afflictions that in most countries were a thing of the past, while I take notes.

1. Measles, polio, tetanus, whooping cough, tuberculosis and diphtheria—referred to as the "six killers."
2. Ordinary diarrhea.

He tosses me a couple of silver packets.

"What's this?"

"Oral rehydration therapy. ORT. A solution made from eight teaspoonsful of sugar and one of salt, mixed in a liter of water. Dehydration resulting from diarrhea accounts for about one third of all child deaths in Sudan."

He tells me that a sachet of ORT costs about seven U.S. cents. The cost of a single Kalashnikov bullet is thirty cents.

"Two hundred thousand children under five die each year in Sudan. Most of the deaths could be avoided through preventative measures. Immunizations. ORT. Safe water and sanitation. Half of all Sudanese children suffer from mild malnutrition, which saps their strength, makes them vulnerable to disease, pneumonia, dysentery, hepatitis. Most problematic are infections due to the traditional methods of Sudanese medicine healers."

3. Polluted water and inadequate sanitation. Typhoid. All kinds of intestinal parasites that "ravage the interior of the body": leishmaniasis; guinea worm; bilharzia (schistosomiasis)/Nile river disease.

"What about cholera?"

"There've been several recent outbreaks. The authorities prefer to call it severe or acute gastroenteritis."

4. Diseases transmitted by flying insects/pests: malaria (stagnant water) and yellow fever (mosquitoes); sleeping sickness, river blindness (fly) . . .

"River blindness?"

"Spread by the bite of black flies that breed in rivers. The infection starts as a painful bump that quickly develops into an itch all over the body. Eventually you go blind."

He moves on to some of the more exotic, often fatal, but hardly rare diseases such as elephantitis, leprosy, yaws, green monkey fever . . .

. . . begins with vomiting, highly contagious, you die.

I'm realizing I'll be lucky to get out of Sudan unscathed.

"I don't want to discourage you, but transport to anywhere outside of Khartoum is a real problem. As is accommodation. Not to mention the lack of food, water, and of course, any type of communication."

He shakes his head. Something is troubling him.

"The problem with you people," he says, referring to the press, "is that you only care about a so-called story when a crisis has been reached. Why is it that people have to be dying to get your attention?"

He pauses. "In fact, people are dying. Not in the proportion of last year's famine, but . . ." He shrugs his shoulders. "Anyway, you'll see for yourself. Do you have any permits yet?"

"No, I just arrived a few hours ago."

He jots down an address for me. "It's open from 6 to 8 p.m." He loads me with fact sheets, booklets, etc., knowing that any media publicity will, even indirectly, be a great help. "Figure out your time schedule and where you want to go, then I'll see how we can assist you. I know you guys generally like to work on your own, but if you want to get anything done here, my only advice is, don't kid yourself. With a deadline like yours, you're going to need all the help you can get."

———

I'm reeling from the confusing array of facts and figures, refugee camps, and diseases. Moreover, the phones are consistently out of order. Exasperated, I sit down at the telex machine, tap out *Newsweek*'s call number, and type a message to Joe Dwyer, the photo editor in charge of the disease story.

PRO DWYER: PLS CONTACT ME. CAN NOW BE REACHED SUDAN HILTON RM
327. PHONE: 74100/78930. TELEX: 22250. NEED TO SPEAK TO YOU BUT
CAN'T SEEM TO GET THROUGH FROM HERE. ITEM: FILM FROM EGYPT
. SHOULD BE ARRIVING ON TWA #801 ETA 15:20 JFK TODAY, BUT PLS CHECK
WITH CAIRO BUREAU. RGDS SPENCER/KHARTOUM.

Like magic, it simultaneously appears in a distant office somewhere else on
this earth. And immediately I feel like an integral part of a larger universe.
Cosmic correspondence. An alien's sense of global belonging.

I finally collapse.

My sleep is interrupted by the sound of something being slipped under
my door.

PRO SPENCER: CAROL, SORRY HAVE BEEN UNABLE TO REACH YOU. HAVE
GIVEN UP AFTER SEVERAL DOZEN TRIES. DON'T KNOW WHAT PROBLEM
YOU FACE, BUT IF MONEY IS IN QUESTION, USE YOUR JUDGMENT, BUT
DON'T GO OVERBOARD. STORY IS LIKELY FOR COMING WEEK. REGARDS,
DWYER.

I reread the telex from *Newsweek,* amused by its content. Photo depart-
ments always worry about money. So do photographers, particularly since
we advance any and all expenses incurred during our assignments. This
includes money spent for hotels, airfares, meals, telexes, phone calls, land
transportation, drivers, fixers, the airfreighting of film, and/or whatever else
might be necessary. In an area like the Middle East, a photographer's out-
lay for a ten-day trip can easily run several thousands of dollars.

For me, cash-flow anxiety is routine, a normal aspect of my day-to-day
working reality, since I cannot bill until after the trip, when I sit down with
an envelope full of receipts and a calculator and feebly attempt to convert
various currencies to dollars at varying exchange rates. The fact that it takes
six to eight weeks before being reimbursed and paid for the actual per di-
ems I have earned strengthens my ability to handle stress. Or so I tell myself. What irks me, however, is the accumulation of interest I've lost over
the years on money advanced for the Fortune 500 publications with whom
I work. And more to the point, the interest they've gained from all of us in
the interim while we risk our lives for the sake of "capturing" specific images that ultimately mean so little.

Never mind. For now, money's not the issue. The problem really, aside
from communications, is travel permits and logistics.

I hurriedly shower and get dressed, not wanting to lose the day. I sit down again with the piles of papers and booklets and maps I now have from UNICEF, the Ministry of Information, the Ministry of Tourism, etc., knowing that I have less than a week to wrap the story. In order to know what permits I will need, I have to figure out where I'm going and how I will get there.

"The connections within the country," the tourist brochure says, "are provided by air, rail, and road services." Then I read in the United Nations booklet that "transport—whether by road, rail, or air—is a tortuous affair." Barely 2 percent of Sudan's roads, including those in urban areas, have tarmac. Secondary roads are a network of dirt tracks, either impassible or quickly washed away in the rains or swept aside in the summer sandstorms.

For instance, the booklet says that "from Khartoum to El Geneina (in the western province about one thousand miles from capital), a Hercules takes two and a half hours; a truck, ten days minimum. From June till September heavy rains make most of western Sudan completely inaccessible: flooding and soft ground make it impossible for trucks and other vehicles. Camel caravans are the only way of getting through."

Fortunately, I am not here during the rainy season. Instead, I will have to contend with "haboobs," the violent windstorms that whip the desert into tornadoes of moving sand, reducing visibility. Not to mention excessive heat. Renting a car is out of the question. I could get lost in the sands, there will be nowhere to fix it if it breaks down, no gas, no decent maps.

Sudan Railways, the booklet continues, "is over-stretched and under-maintained. Most routes are antiquated and insufficient, trains are subject to breakdowns, and the single-track railway line suffers frequent washouts during the rainy season. All services suffer from a shortage of fuel, spare parts, and funds to maintain equipment."

Sudan Air, the state-owned domestic carrier, is a sort of cistern in which all the chaos of the nation is collected. Planes routinely skip stops, make unplanned layovers of several days, leave without passengers, or most commonly, don't leave at all. The airline is renowned for maintenance problems. It becomes clear that if I am to get anywhere, I'll have to hitch a ride with one of the relief agencies.

I spend the entire day dealing with various governmental bureaucracies. First, the Ministry of Information for press credentials; otherwise, I may run into problems when I'm taking pictures. Then, the Ministry of Interior for travel permits; otherwise, I'm not allowed to leave Khartoum. The travel documents must be stamped at the "Aliens" office. The Aliens office, which looks like a rundown rural post office, says to come back on Saturday. Today is only Thursday. I can't lose the time. A bribe passes hands. My documents are stamped and received one hour later. I return to the Ministry of Interior so that the stamped travel papers can now be signed; if not, they're considered invalid. Next, I visit the office of the Sudanese Commission for Refugees. I need authorization, which comes in the form of formal letters of permission, in order to visit specific refugee camps. At each of these offices, I must explain why I am here, exactly what it is I will be doing, and provide several passport pictures.

By the end of the day, which in this heat is 2 p.m., miraculously, I have all the papers, documents, letters, and press cards that I need in order to work. I have dinner with the director of the Save the Children Fund to coordinate a program with their field staff in eastern Sudan. Only then do I find out that the type of malaria pills I'm taking are completely worthless.

———

PRO DWYER URGENT: ANYONE HOME? PLS GIVE DWYER MESSAGE. COM-
MUNICATIONS IMPOSSIBLE HERE AND MUST SPEAK ASAP. I CANNOT PHONE
FROM HERE. PLS CONTACT ME. REPEAT. CANNOT GET THROUGH BY
PHONE. PLS CONTACT SPENCER IN SUDAN. ITEM: SUDAN HOLDING ELEC-
TIONS NEXT WEEK, FIRST IN 18 YEARS. LET ME KNOW IF YOU WANT PIX.

24

Wau (Wow!)

(MARCH 1986)

At 4 a.m. Friday morning, twelve bleary-eyed foreign correspondents assemble at Khartoum Airport. World Vision, an international relief organization, has organized a small charter to fly us into southern Sudan, scene of an ongoing civil war. We would be landing in Wau, one of the few towns not yet captured by the rebel guerrillas of the Sudanese People's Liberation Army (SPLA). Cut off from food and medical supplies, the people of Wau are facing starvation, and relief planes are scarce as the SPLA is attempting to shoot down anything that flies over its territory.

Several hours later, our plane skids to a halt on a barely discernible airstrip. While the reporters are chauffeured to their interviews, Marc Fletcher and I take to the dirt paths of Wau on his battered relief worker's motorbike, looking for pictures. I hold tightly to the hollowed bones of his malaria-ridden body, trying to balance myself and the weight of my camera bag so we won't tip over. We travel the outskirts of Wau through modest hamlets of sun-dried, circular, mud-gray huts, daydreaming to the echo of African drumbeats. When the mood is upon us, we stop and take pictures.

Together we cover a lot of ground, the sun beaming down on that long, narrow stretch of bumpy, beaten earth to which we lose ourselves for a spell. Along the way, we discover a leper colony and coax bashful smiles from fragmented forms. A few hours later, we are surrounded with the laughter of tribal Sudanese children as we photograph the seductive ballet of a fevered woman dancing to the rhythm of her African soul. Amid the solemn line of a thousand ragged refugees, her impassioned whirls loom out of context like a disordered medley. I spend an hour or so shooting, in case *Newsweek* cares about the story, in case the public cares about starving Africans, in case anyone cares about civil war in a town called Wau.

Mid-afternoon we scan the town for something to eat until the husky resonance of blaring reggae beckons us from a threadbare joint with colossal tin speakers. It is 114 degrees outside when we leave to chat up soldiers at the government army base, hoping to charm them into some military-type pictures. For that we are almost arrested. Afterward, at dusk, we wander through the hamlets looking for home-brewed apple beer, and then rush "home" breathlessly, having run out of gas only minutes before the hushed hour of curfew sets in.

Our group has been given an abandoned house, and in the evening we sit for hours around the oval dining table swapping stories and newsroom gossip. Sometimes the uniform crunch of soldiers on foot patrol prompts remarks about the guerrilla-held war zone. Late into the night we finally retire. The women commandeer the only bedroom, the men sprawl out on cushions across the living room floor.

It is about 3:30 in the morning when an explosion shakes me from a deep sleep.

"It's a bomb," says the *New York Times* reporter.

"No, I think it's a landmine," says the Associated Press reporter.

We continue listening for a few minutes, but since nothing follows but a heavy stillness, we slump back down into our missionary cots, covering our heads with pillows.

We wake up early in the morning to the sound of distinctly boyish laughter. Curious, we stroll into the living room to a barrage of obvious zeal and are unmercifully teased for our middle-of-the-night speculations.

"So, what was it then?" I ask.

"Mangoes," says the *Newsweek* correspondent.

"Oh come on, Ray. Be serious."

"He's telling you the truth, Carol," Fletcher says. "Come outside and we'll prove it."

With that the guys, still chuckling, march outside, the three of us wondering what possible trick they have conjured up during some restless hour. Ray takes a large mango that had fallen off the tree partially draping over the house, tosses it high up into the air so it will drop back down onto the tin roof. The impact is deafening.

Mango grenades. The latest invention in unconventional guerrilla war tactics.

We leave in the early afternoon. Marc Fletcher stays behind to help distribute the food and medical supplies that World Vision has brought down with us. Halfway into our return flight, an emergency bulletin comes over the pilot's radio. A plane chartered by Save the Children has disappeared somewhere in the vicinity over which we are flying. Would we please try to spot it? All eyes strain over the massive sun-bleached desert, but the plane has vanished as if curtly seized by God's holy hand. Like Fletcher, the volunteers aboard were typical relief workers: selfless, dedicated, trusting, heroic. They are not mentioned in the reporters' stories.

The cover that could have been: Terrorists in training, Lebanon, 1986.

Arab boy with sheep.

Muammar Qadhafi, president of Libya, 1984.

Old Jerusalem, Orthodox Jews, July 1986.

Carol looking out over Jerusalem.

Carol at work.

Two Bedouins in the desert.

Abu Iyad, November 1984, head of Fatah's security and intelligence,
chief of PLO's Black September Organization; he personally authorized the Munich
operation that resulted in the massacre of eleven Israeli athletes.

Landscape—Carol's feeling for place.

Yasser Arafat at the 1984 PLO conference in Jordan.

Arafat with some of his cronies.

Arafat praying.

At the Rafah border—families separated by a fence, 1984.

Girls at Gaza Beach Elementary School, December 1984.

Gaza refugee camp, 1986.

Woman and son, Shatila camp, 1984.

Old woman in Gaza, Shatila camp, 1984.

King Hussein with his ham radio, 1988.

King Hussein with Sheik Zayed of United Arab Emirates, August 15, 1986.

King Hussein in his airplane.

King Hussein with Queen Noor, 1985.

Demonstration in Gaza.

Bringing coffins and bodies home.

Newsweek

Photographer Carol Spencer   Color

Date 5/18/85   For Overseas/International   B & W ✓

Department Photo/World   Rolls

Development ※ TWA Hostage Story ※

Use separate envelopes for color and B & W film.
Key captions and processing to roll numbers.

Roll
No.   GIVE COMPLETE CAPTIONS

Dorothy Sullivan, describing her ordeal on the hijacked plane, after arriving in Cyprus. Sullivan was among the first group of 19 hostages released in Beruit, and flown to Cyprus.

Do Not Fold — Negatives Enclosed

Newsweek form that Carol used to send film in.

PLO training camp, Lebanon, 1986.

Press madness, TWA, 1985.

Arafat, left, with Abu Jihad, far right, 1985.
(Abu Jihad is the father of the holy war, one of the Fatah founders).

Boy with gun and dog tags, PLO camp, Lebanon, 1986.

Girl with gun, PLO camp, Lebanon, 1986.

Faces covered, learning to ambush, PLO camp, Lebanon, 1986.

Palestinian soldiers relaxing.

Lebanon, 1986.

Kids somersaulting in camp formations, PLO camp, Lebanon, 1986.

Tuberculosis victim, Sudan, 1986.

Leprosy victim, Sudan, 1986.

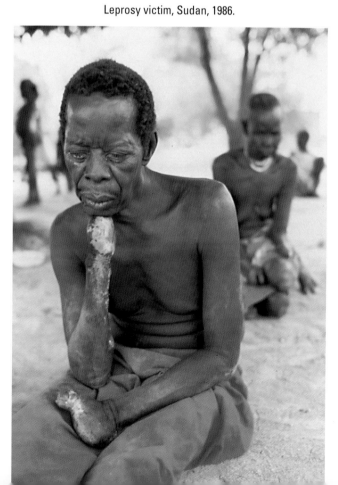

Woman and child, Sudan, 1986.

Gaza rubble.

Starving boy, Sudan, 1986.

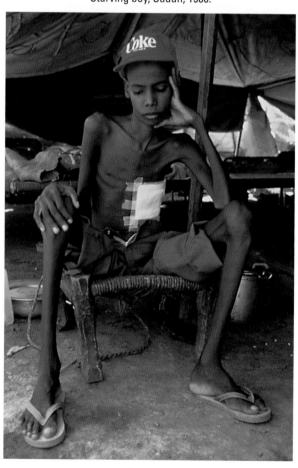

Egypt's Anwar Sadat, 1985.

Shimon Peres, Bill Clinton, and King Hussein.

Shimon Peres and Margaret Thatcher.

George H. W. Bush and Hosni Mubarak.

Petra, Jordan.

I Don't Know What I'm Feeling

(APRIL 1986)

ATTN: STUART WILLCUTS/WORLD VISION

STUART: MANY THANX FOR WONDERLAND OF WAU. SUPERB TRIP BUT AS
PROPHESIZED, NEWSWEEK WENT WIRE. BY THE WAY, ANY POSSIBILITY
YOU MIGHT BE ABLE TO HELP WITH ETHIOPIAN VISA?
PLS LET ME KNOW. RGDS, CAROL.

PRO SPENCER FROM WILLCUTS

CAROL: CURRENT SITUATION REGARDING ETHIOPIAN VISAS QUITE UN-
CERTAIN. GOV NOT GIVING THEM OUT THESE DAYS UNTIL DUST SETTLES.
SORRY CAN'T BE OF ASSISTANCE. TRUST YOU GOT WORD ABOUT FLETCH-
ER'S PLANE BEING SHOT DOWN. YOU WILL RECALL, FLETCHER WAS RE-
LIEF VOLUNTEER STAYING WITH US AT HOUSE IN WAU. HOPE TO SEE YOU
SOMETIME. RGDS, STUART.

I try to figure out if the news of Marc's death touches me. It frightens me
that I actually must pause to think about this. Nothing in particular comes
to mind except that it could just as easily have been any one of us scattered somewhere amid the shifting sands of Sudan. I replay the twenty-four
hours Fletcher and I spent together as if time were a video with automatic
controls, but all I see are transient images that might make a cover. I push
the search mechanism to ferret out the scene that might make me cry, that
might force me to acknowledge whatever it is I'm feeling. But I have only
the sense of a voyeur standing apart, creating images out of the life before
me. I compose the moment; I don't have to feel it. Click. Snap.

Maybe I've seen too much. We move about like a swarm of bees gathering pollen. An existence whose substance centers around hardcore

headline news, half-packed duffel bags, airline schedules, hotel rooms, a Sony nine-band radio, and the bars journalists always hang out in. After a while, values begin to dissipate. Editorial biases intervene. Motivation is reduced to getting a front-page story or a cover photograph. This is our center of gravity, the nucleus of our survival. Truths are skillfully manipulated. Stories hyped. The captions of pictures altered. Friends and colleagues die. Hacks turn into alcoholics. Marriages break up. Affairs are part of the diet. Life, stitched together from notable bylines. You learn to snatch the moment. There might not be another.

And yet, as much as I hate the news, there's nothing quite like that rush of a "good" story . . .

Sometimes when I've been up too late having trouble falling asleep, I organize the details of my funeral the way most women plan their wedding.

GUEST LIST: Small

TYPE OF FLOWERS: Pastels with a touch of purple — no roses

MUSIC: Nina Simone: "Just Like A Woman," "Do Whatcha Gotta Do"; Tina Turner: "What's Love Got to Do with It"; Ray Charles: "Just Because"

WORDS: Rainer Maria Rilke; Ai; Primo Levi

Outdoor barbeque, lots of chaos

LOCATION: Unknown

Dammit, Fletcher . . .

A penny for your last thoughts. You never talked about yourself. Why did you isolate yourself in a town that nobody even cares about? You were the only volunteer left. Didn't you have anyone to go back to? I thought about sending your parents a note, but it was too much trouble to find out where you live. Were you hit with a shoulder-held, Soviet-made surface-to-air missile?

The eulogy is what I have the most problems with.

I think about the waves of emotions I've muddled through over the years. I think about the moments I've been proud of—overcoming fears, staying with something those extra few minutes, trying my best to offer love—unpublished moments. I think about the choices I've made and wonder how it might have been different. I think about how I've changed and whether anyone noticed. I think about these things and know that I want someone to speak about what I still hoped for rather than what I did; not about who I was, but rather that I cherished the adventure of trying to become. And if I seemed stubborn or selfish or headstrong, mention that I was afraid not of death, but of drifting into nothingness, of living my life within the static frame of society's image.

Young photographers, with their hungry eyes and brazen talk, rush off with the same earnestness, integrity, and exuberance. You learn to toughen up, expect less, notice more, until one day the madness of an unpredictable moment blurs your sure-shot vision, and suddenly you ask yourself: "What am I doing here? What the hell am I doing?" The moment fades but the feeling lingers, disquieting as a subliminal stammer. Everything's negotiable at the right price, even life. "Danger pay," the invoice says. Double day rate—a photographer's war-zone value.

26

You Need Something to Peg the Story On

(APRIL 1986)

PRO SPENCER: ALL CIRCUITS TO SUDAN HAVE BEEN JAMMED AND I AM UNABLE TO REACH YOU BY PHONE AT THIS POINT. WILL TRY AGAIN LATER. RGDS. DWYER. P.S. YOU HAVE COVER THIS WEEK ON TERROR AND I HAVEN'T LOOKED AT YOUR DISEASE SHOOT YET BUT A QUICK GLANCE AT THE BANDW CONTACTS LOOKED GOOD.

CAROL: HAPPY BIRTHDAY. WE TRIED TO CALL YOU BUT NO LINES. WE ALL LOVE YOU AND MISS YOU. LOVE DAD, SUE, AND SUSAN.

PRO SPENCER: HAD A CALL FROM YOUR DAD WHO WOULD LIKE YOU TO CALL HIM WHEN YOU GET A CHANCE. ITEM: NEWSWEEK'S NAIROBI BU-REAU CHIEF RAY WILKINSON ARRIVING ON SUNDAY AND WILL LOOK FOR YOU. P.S. BELIEVE YOU HAVE ALL COVERS. RGDS/DWYER

CAROL: RCV'D YOUR TWIX. HAPPY BIRTHDAY. CONGRATULATIONS. YOU HAVE COVER OF NEWSWEEK THIS WEEK. PROUD OF YOU BUT MISS YOU. LOVE, DAD.

PRO DWYER/NEWSWEEK PHOTO NY URGENT
JOE: LOGISTICS OF GETTING DISEASE FILM TO NY ON TIME, DIFFICULT TO SAY THE LEAST. IF STORY STILL SCHEDULED, BEST BET FOR ME TO HAND-CARRY TO CAIRO TONIGHT AND THEN SHIP FILM ON AIR FRANCE FLIGHT DEP. CAIRO 10:40 AM THURS FOR PARIS. PARIS BUREAU COULD THEN SEND PACKAGE ON CONCORDE ARRIVING NY 830AM FRIDAY.
HAVE TELEX HERE THAT I SHOULD LEAVE TOMORROW FOR SOUTHERN SU-DAN SO PLEASE ADVISE WHAT YOU WANT ME TO DO.

There are things that can happen to a photographer's pictures. Film can miss its flight connections or get held up in customs just long enough to arrive too late for one's deadline. Stories can get killed. And always there is the competition of other photographers whose pictures are sent to the magazine you are working for and, for one reason or another, an editor decides to use their picture instead of yours because they like the angle better or whatever.

You learn to roll with the punches, do the best that you can, and hopefully not take it all too seriously. But most of the time, somewhat miraculously, everything goes according to plan. You get the pictures you need. Your film makes all of its airline connections. The story that you worked on runs. The following week as you flip through the magazine, the results of your own personal efforts are right there in the form of a published photograph.

———

You need something to peg the story on. The words keep repeating themselves in my head. How many times have I heard them? When was the first time? What does it really mean?

My thirty-second birthday, in Sudan. I find out I have Newsweek's "Inside Terror" cover. The story was "held" for two months. It is the U.S. bombing of Libya that provides the "peg" for the story.

The "disease shoot" does make it to New York on time, but at the last minute, the story is killed. It sits in New York in a cardboard box under the editor's feet for eight months, and then is used as an adjunct to a cover story on AIDS.

PART 6

The Striptease

LOCATION/YEAR: GAZA STRIP, WEST BANK, JERUSALEM;
1987–1989

When I have a camera
in my hand, I know no fear.

—ALFRED EISENSTAEDT

27

Everybody Must Get Stoned

(DECEMBER 1987)

We are not there when it begins, so I cannot tell you exactly how it happened. No one in the foreign press corps anticipated that the "disturbances" reported in Jabalia, the largest Palestinian refugee camp in the Gaza Strip, would blaze into mass riots and rage. Can a picture of that day be recreated by words alone?

Throughout the camp, thick pillars of smoke from burning tires blacken the Mediterranean sky above the swell of corrugated tin roofs. Blue-jean–clad youth, their faces wrapped in checkered masks, swarm in and out of sniper focus, taunting the Israeli army as they whistle "*Jihad*." In their hands they clench the weapons by which this insurrection will be remembered: the stones that they hope will change their fate in unknown and perhaps mythical ways.

Mothers and wives robed in ankle-length coarse black cottons, intricately embroidered across the chest, surge into the scorched air to scream at the khaki green soldiers who symbolize their exile and are swept away in the acrid haze of tear gas. "It's better to die than to go on like this," one woman yells.

Crowds of Palestinians, who were banished from their homes and land, line the alleys of filth-mottled sand. Even the children strut out from their graying, patched-up huts to throw stones at the army patrols, willing to blow themselves away so as not to have their world forgotten.

It happens so quickly.

The boy barely has time to feel the first bullet hit his shoulder. When the second bullet enters his chest, nothing can save him. His bloodied body is shouldered high above the dust-powdered streets, suddenly detached, torn away from the others. His life slipped away, unpublished, yet his death stamps the birth date of the revolution that became known throughout the world as "the intifada."

HATEM MOHAMMED YOUSEF SISSI

BORN IN 1972 IN JABALIA REFUGEE CAMP, GAZA STRIP

DIED A *shaheed*, MARTYR, DECEMBER 9, 1987

Things are nasty in the Strip.

By the time I arrive, even the head doctor at nearby Shifa Hospital, Gaza's largest medical center, shrugs his shoulders. "I can't promise you're safe here," he says.

I mumble something about my job as a photojournalist. Outside, a mob of angry Palestinian youth barricades the hospital's main entrance while Israeli soldiers encircle the building.

I poke my head out a side door to see what is happening. In the parking lot, right in front of me, three university-aged women in the gray dress and white scarves of Islamists are hatcheting the pavement to pieces. The women fill translucent bags with chunks of concrete and hand them to their masked comrades at the front, assembly-line style. I duck back inside, out of sight. It is a delicate moment, maybe dangerous. I can't resist. I step outside and begin snapping pictures, a decision that proves to be foolhardy.

The masked men spin around, turning their backs to the soldiers, and pitch chunks of black pavement at me. I sprint back through the hospital lobby, but smatterings of glass and concrete break up around me as chunks tumble and fall. The mob chases me, shouting, "Yahudi, Yahudi!"

I am surrounded, stones coming at my head, dozens of fists clasping rocks with jagged edges, faces swathed except for the pairs of huge brown eyes gone wild, white and rabid, rimmed with madness, contorted with rage. My Nikons are battered. I think I will die, when one of the men slings me toward the wall, then wraps his arms around me, shielding me with his own body. He shoves me into an empty examination room. The door slams shut, then this same man, whose face I can't see, and whose name I'll never know, whispers a muffled apology and demands I give him my film. Which I do.

———

The following day I'm bathing my bruises, and my mother calls from the United States. She sounds relieved. "I'm glad it's you," she says. "I just heard the news on NBC. I was worried."

She tells me two American journalists have been kidnapped at a hospital

in Gaza, and Palestinians are threatening to kill them. I reply that it is probably just a rumor, but she says it must be true. After all, it was reported on
television.

"Are you all right?" she asks, sensing I'm not.

"I'm okay, just a little tired."

Journalists, especially the cameramen, are plastering their cars with signs
written in English and Arabic that say "Foreign Press," hoping we'll be im-
mune from the stones. Photographers have it particularly rough. Those
who get too close to the action on the Palestinian side either have rocks
hurled at them or else find themselves so overcome by tear gas that they
can't film anyway. If you try to go off the beaten track, perhaps into the back
streets of one of the camps, you run a high risk of being assaulted.

Gaza's Palestinians don't like photojournalists. They are convinced we
hand over our film to the Shin Bet, the Israeli secret police, so Palestinian
rioters can be identified. Their fear is understandable if you know plain-
clothed Shin Bet agents are posing as photographers for exactly this purpose, a deception that angers the "real" photographers. After all, we are
there to take pictures. But even if we are bona fide foreign press, how can
the Palestinians be sure we will not frame their activists?

"You make us look like animals," I am told repeatedly.

They aren't fools. Our limited coverage of the Strip has been reduced to
symbolic duels, and the duels to a blood feud: Davids and Goliaths, Arabs
and Jews.

Such imagery perpetuates a profoundly simplistic impression of their
lives. While the strife implicit in endless photos of "guns against stones"
successfully dramatizes daily demonstrations, the gladiatorial image does
little to explain the nagging problems of existence for the 700,000 residents
of the Strip, trapped in an unbearable gray zone, where even the citizenship
of those lucky enough to have travel documents is listed as "undefined."

I think of Yasser Arafat's business card, with just a name, no address, no
telephone, no place to call home.

28

Photo-Realism, the "Real" Picture, and the Ingathering

(DECEMBER 1987)

I sit in my hotel room in Gaza, thinking about a phone conversation I've just had with an editor at *U.S. News & World Report* magazine.

"We thought for a different picture, maybe you could photograph the funeral of the Palestinian that was shot?" he said.

"Which one?" I asked.

"You know, the teenager."

"Oh, you mean in Gaza. No. I'm sorry. There haven't been any public funerals for Palestinians for a year, maybe longer. I'm not even sure what happens to the bodies. The Israeli army usually spirits the dead away, they say, to perform an autopsy. But according to the family, sometimes the corpse just disappears. Or if the body is returned, which seems to only happen in the middle of the night, a funeral might be allowed then and there, with only the immediate family present."

"You mean the pictures we see of women grieving are taken spontaneously?" he asked.

"I'm not sure you understand what's happening here."

"Well, maybe you can get something that shows grief. You know, like women crying."

"Sure. No problem," I said, reminding myself that photographers are hired to illustrate "the News," not to tell an editor what "the News" really is. We look for what we know is publishable, look for certain elements: gun, keffiyeh, youth . . . We're not to comment on the images our cameras have recorded, the scenes to which we have been witness. We just have to prove the story, or the magazine's version of the story for that particular week. Our photographs are published; our thoughts—and captions—are not.

Over time, we stop seeing the whole, everything else around us. Our own vision becomes blinkered, which is also true for the photo editors who sort through the images. There's a contradiction between truth and beauty, and a photo is really about aesthetics, isn't it?

I think of *Time's* first cover photograph on the Palestinian uprising. In the picture, someone's eyes stare back at me. He is unidentified, anonymous, masked, his face tightly wrapped in the black, red, white, and green colors of the Palestinian flag, as if it were a keffiyeh. The caption for the cover image reads "Photograph of Palestinian demonstrator in the Gaza Strip."

Who would have surmised that this photograph is a figment of someone's imagination, the caption invented and the portrait "created" because of an out-of-town editor's or photographer's preconceived idea? In real life, the Palestinian flag is not worn as a keffiyeh. Never. It's just not done. But most probably, no one would know the difference, unless, of course, you happen to live here.

———

During a Friday evening dinner party at an American reporter's home in Jerusalem, the press is obsessed with "the story." The host, Robert Ruby, has invited a dozen or so American and British journalists whose beat is the Middle East. Dress is casual, the average age early to mid-thirties, and men outnumber women four-to-one.

The living room, where everyone has gathered to unscramble the day's events, is dominated by wall-to-wall shelves of prominently displayed hardcover books by Tom Wolfe, Gay Talese, Hunter S. Thompson, and George Plimpton. The intifada, still in its first weeks, is the only topic of conversation.

MARY: You wouldn't believe Gaza today. It was like an inferno. The whole town was burning, even in the upper-class streets. (She shakes her bobbed brown hair in disbelief, then continues slowly in a midwestern drawl.) I was in this lawyer's home when tear gas started to drift. His seven-year-old son says, "Damn those soldiers," and then calmly walks through the house shutting all of the windows. It was amazing. He knew exactly what to do.

COLLIN (studying Mary's face): Anyone killed?

MARY: I saw one person shot, twice in the legs. An eighty-six-year-old man.

COLLIN (surprised): How do you know he was eighty-six?

MARY (emphatically): Because the family I was talking to knew him. They said he was born in 1902.

PAUL (in a vaguely condescending tone): Come on . . . Palestinians never know when they're born.

MARK (the newest correspondent to have arrived in the region, pouring himself a beer): Was it live ammunition or rubber bullets?

CAROL (the only photographer present, lighting a cigarette, frowning): You mean rubber-coated bullets. You know they have metal pellets inside.

MARK: That's what propels them.

CAROL: Did you hear about Ala, the five-year-old boy from Nablus? He was shot in the head with a so-called rubber bullet two days ago and is still in intensive care. He doesn't even recognize his own family.

JUDY (twirling the ice in her drink): I hear they were using dum-dum bullets in Gaza today.

ROD (to Judy): The IDF denied it.

JUDY (to Rod): But the doctors at Shifa Hospital confirmed it.

(Then there is an argument as to whether dum-dum bullets are the ones that burst to smithereens once they're lodged in the body or simultaneously twist as they spiral through.)

TED: Does anyone know the casualty count today?

DAVID: The IDF said five wounded. But that was a few hours ago.

CHARLES: No deaths?

PAUL: Not reported.

MARY: The Palestinian Press Service said at least twenty-two were wounded.

MARK: I guess that means about twelve.

JUDY: Does that include beatings?

COLLIN: No.

CAROL (quietly, as if to herself): What's happening in this country? Did you hear Abba Eban lately? He's been calling the new beating policy "Operation Bone-Breaker."

(Three weeks after this conversation, Rami Abdel Aklouk, a fifteen-year-old refugee from the Gaza Strip, will receive a blow to his head from a wooden truncheon that is so harsh, so profound, the boy will become known as the first person to be beaten to death by an Israeli soldier. The "beating" will occur as Rami is riding home from the vegetable market on his father's donkey cart.)

PAUL (over the ring of the telephone): Don't you get tired of the Israelis saying that we're exaggerating the situation and that the media's to blame for the outbreak of spontaneous riots?

ROD: Or that the problem is not the Palestinians, but the state of war with the Arab states.

CAROL (sighing): What I'm sick of is the Palestinians accusing us of being spies for the Shin Bet, and demanding to see our foreign press cards.

MARK (deliberately changing the subject): I was in Anata refugee camp this morning—

MARY: Anata's a neighborhood, not a camp.

MARK (angrily): I'm telling you, I was there and it's a camp.

MARY (placating): The camp's called Shu'fat; Anata's the neighborhood next to it.

MARK: No, it's the other way around. (He stares at her for a moment and says nothing, then shrugs, his face grim.) This place is like a hall of mirrors. I've never been so confused about a story in my life.

———

Fourteen months after the start of the intifada, the Strip is neglected by most journalists and abandoned by nearly all foreign camerapeople. Yet the rebellion continues.

According to the United Nations Relief and Works Agency for Palestinian Refugees (UNRWA), between December 9, 1987 (when the street riots began), and February 28, 1989, 117 Gazans have died; 15,557 have been injured (94 Gazans died from gunshot wounds by live ammunition; 2 from plastic-coated metal bullets; 13 from asphyxiation by tear gas; and 8 from beatings; 1,840 Gazans were injured by live ammunition; 1,019 by rubber bullets; 314 by plastic-coated metal bullets; 3,665 as a result of tear gas; and 8,709 as a result of beatings). Thousands of others have been arrested, intimidated, detained, and placed under house arrest.

What does this suggest, and why is it important?

It suggests, in part, our inability to perceive the experience of Gaza's Palestinians; that there is a gap that exists between "the story" in journalistic terms and the story of "real life." Put differently, journalists have yet to define the question: What is the intifada about? We are unable to deal with the fact that the "uprising"—as the foreign press corps is prone to call the intifada—is a grassroots revolution; that the revolution began because of an identity crisis; and that the crisis evolved out of the struggle to maintain, or perhaps affirm, the reality of an Arab Palestinian people who had been made to feel like impostors, outsiders who are potentially a threat, the painted birds who don't belong.

This question of reality-maintenance is central to understanding what was happening in "the Strip." Consider the following report published in the February 28 edition of the *Jerusalem Post*, Israel's English language daily: "Army patrols in Gaza have been trying to combat the new fashion of sweatshirts decorated with the black Palestinian checkered design."

And think about what it must mean to a Palestinian refugee who is also a teenager.

29

The Striptease

(JULY 1990)

The *Washington Post's* photo editor calls to ask if I am interested in shoot-ing a project the newspaper is planning on the Gaza Strip. The offer is en-ticing, a chance to get away from the imagery of cliché. Yet I am reluctant to take on the assignment.

Between June 1950 and June 1990, the refugee population in the Strip has grown from 198,227 people to 496,339, more than half of whom live in eight camps that were set up temporarily for displaced Palestinians and are now permanent sites. This one statistic gives some idea of the vast number of Palestinians stripped of their belongings, who are trying to come to terms with the loss of their property and with the unenviable position of "being here" in Gaza, instead of "over there," in what is now the State of Israel.

It has taken me years to digest just how tangled the refugee situation ac-tually is, to comprehend the discontentment born of a life muddled by po-litical limbo, stateless and homeless without having lost country or home, and to have the memory of a past life that has been rigidly fixed in the minds of the children, blurring the edges of reality, as hope in the present has faded into a future without form. Can this be captured in a series of photographs?

All of which gnaws at my psyche now as I think about how to photo-graph this complex place and reproduce what it means to live in the Strip. As a friend asked, "Does a photographer's gaze gratuitously 'reproduce' the 'experience'?"

On top of which, taking pictures will be difficult. The intifada violence has now turned inward with the phenomenon of collaborators and the murder of Palestinians by other Palestinians. The *shabiba*, hooded masked youth who had taken on the Israeli army at the beginning of the intifada, now control the streets, terrorizing in the name of "purifying" Palestinian society. Known and suspected collaborators are murdered, and their corpses sometimes dismembered. Drug dealers, criminals, prostitutes, and men and women whose behavior is alleged to be "immoral" are beaten to death with stones and iron rods, lynched, slashed, and stabbed with knives, daggers, and axes, the bellies of pregnant women slit open. None of which can be filmed, adding to the population's facelessness. There's been a spate of articles in the Arab press condemning the brutal, unwarranted killings, but for the most part, none of this makes the evening news. If there are no images, it's as if it didn't happen. It's out of control, so much so that a well-known Palestinian journalist recently warned that "the revolution is the phantom starting to eat its children." There's a good chance I'll be physically attacked.

My decision of whether to accept the assignment is made for me by Iraq's invasion of Kuwait. The project on the Strip is abruptly abandoned as the entire foreign press corps dogs Saddam and "Stormin' Norman" in the Gulf.

PART 7

The Mother of All Battles

LOCATION/YEAR: THE WEST BANK, ISRAEL;
FALL/WINTER 1990–1991

Man and war: it shapes
his psychology, his outlook,
and his patterns of thought.
Once experienced, war never
ends: he will always think
in its images, imposing
them on each new reality—
a reality from which he is
always partly estranged.
Reality is time-present, but
he is possessed by time-past,
constantly returning to what
he has lived through and how
he survived it. His thinking
is obsessively repeating,
obsessively retrospective.
—RYSZARD KAPUSCINSKI

Today's news wraps
tomorrow's fish.
—JEWISH PROVERB

30

What the Hell Am I Doing?

(DECEMBER 1990)

It's Christmas morning on the West Bank and since I have no family here with which to celebrate, I'm facing the question I've been putting off since Iraq invaded Kuwait four months ago. But with Iraqi Scud missiles hurtling over the desert, it's time to decide—am I better off staying put in Beit Jala or should I move back to Jerusalem? My eyes scan the cover of the current issue of *Time* lying on the coffee table: "What Is Kuwait? And Is It Worth Dying For?" (Dec. 24)

I call an Israeli friend and ask him if I'm being paranoid. He tells me he's just finished cleaning out and equipping his bomb shelter.

"Oh, what am I supposed to take?" I ask. I hadn't gotten that far in my thinking.

"My children could tell you that," he says. His kids are ages three and six.

I write as he dictates a list: candles, matches, battery-operated flashlight and radio, water, canned food, sweets . . .

"Why sweets?" I say.

"To have something you enjoy."

. . . bottle opener, can opener, blankets, toilet paper, a bucket, a heavy jacket (it's cold this time of year), garbage bags, a couple of books, a chair or two, a mattress if possible, maybe a little table. I add on dog/cat food, a litter box.

I hang up and then I wonder, but what if it's a gas attack? And how will we know?

I go to the closet and take out my gas mask. I think of the irony of giving gas masks to people in the territories, a population that has proclaimed Israel an enemy and that supports Saddam. They petitioned Israel's high court for distribution of masks and won.

At 6:20 p.m., it is nearly five days since the war began. No one is outside. I switch on the lights, the radio, and the TV, thinking how eerie it feels to be one of 5 million people locked into their homes, obsessed by Saddam's threat to incinerate Israel, while hundreds of foreign journalists are caught up in their own routine. This evening, for instance, they are floating around the Hilton. The bar is jammed with people drinking beer and whiskey, watching each other, nicotine choking the air, waiting for the next scenario, compelled by adrenaline and the romance of danger. The foreign press streamed into Israel, waiting for something to happen, spectators who come and go, the most macho of whom are in Tel Aviv because that is where it will happen. Those who are based here have sent their families out. They've moved into hotels where the "press centers" are but really for the comfort of being together.

When Iraq first invaded Kuwait, *Newsweek* called and asked me to travel to Jordan immediately to shoot an exclusive story on King Hussein. For the first time in my career, I refused to accept the assignment, because I knew the king would be put into a black box, because of the spin I knew *Newsweek* would put on the story. In the U.S. administration's eyes, he had failed to side with the West. I also knew he was in an impossible situation.

Similarly, tonight I have no desire to join my colleagues. A chasm now exists in the reality that I once shared with them, and although the stories we covered together are my most memorable experiences, they also seem so fictitious, so far removed from what I have come to believe as reality, that lately I have begun to feel a crisis of consciousness. After twenty years of taking pictures—fourteen years professionally—almost everything I've done seems make-believe. It's strange, but lately I've begun to feel like a victim of my own framing.

Tonight I prefer to live through the reality of the war without my cameras, to experience how patterns of behavior change. I sleep with my clothes on. If I go outside, my first thought is, do I have my gas mask and radio? I'm glued to the TV. I'm alert to sounds in a country where the sonic booms of fighter jets regularly disrupt quietude. And I'm afraid. Not so much for myself, but that something may happen to someone I know.

My family has been calling me, begging me to come home. You don't have to be there, they say. But I do have to be here. I justify it by saying that clearly this will be the epilogue to my book, justifying the title *Danger Pay*, after the amount a photographer gets paid when working in a war zone. Except that I am not covering this war. Instead, I want to live through it, see it without my cameras.

I make a habit of filling up my house with flowers. It makes me feel at home, though there's no one here but myself. It's my home filled with my presence. Well, almost—for instinct like a guide has ushered in a companion. It's my solitude that's come to greet me again, and I've decided to let it stay.

Solitude is a nag. It insists on shadowing me everywhere, chattering away in a thousand different voices, bugging me about all sorts of things. I sometimes feel that solitude thinks my life needs certain modifications, despite whatever I may believe. Last week, for instance, solitude marched me to a pet store and, before I quite knew what happened, I came home carrying a cat, a Persian with the face of an owl. How can I have an animal with the way I travel? But solitude says: "What kind of life is this, without anyone to take care of but yourself?" Now, when I get lonely, the cat and I play hide-and-seek, sprinting about the stone floors like kids at a dance. Solitude doesn't join us, just watches with a lopsided grin, terribly pleased with itself. I fear that solitude may become indispensable, for under its influence I am beginning to see things in an entirely new way. And even more frightening is the recognition that this is possible.

It's the hour of twilight that I dread the most. The same hour that as a photographer I've always loved. I lurch through second gear, thinking about how with darkness comes a perverse theater that could be a film or dream, or a live freak show. The streets of Jerusalem are already empty, the shops and cafes closed. The stars glitter overhead, and for a moment I remember how easy it once was to impose order on appearance, make it firm. In fear the senses slip away, like light dimming into the black canvas of night. Everyone waits for the howl of an air-raid siren.

A stunning moon holds my eye. I stand in front of my home, listening to the wind. The air has me in its grip. Wait, I hear myself whisper. There is an image here, still out of focus and indistinguishable from the background, lacking contour and hue. It is not something that can be framed in the here-and-now. It has to be defined from another angle, constructed with hindsight through the work of memory, talked over and explored in depth.

My thoughts sink into the evening's hidden depths. It is silent everywhere now. People say that images speak for themselves. They take for granted that the camera can reveal something that one person saw and another did not; that a picture doesn't lie. They forget that when a photographer creates an image, the flow of time passing has been arrested.

I close my eyes, and when I open them the wind lifts me into the past across a stepping-stone path of still photographs. If symbols play a role in the subconscious, then this is not nostalgia. But symbols can only go so far, unless they remain open to interpretation. To grapple with their subtle form is to grasp the deeper layers of making the image itself. It is thought to be an easy matter to distinguish between reality and appearance, fact and fiction. In covering the news, this is extremely difficult, especially in the Middle East. When the personal encroaches upon the world of the perceiver, particularly during a state of war, the complexities defy conventional notions.

31

The Sealed Room

(DECEMBER 1990)

When I hear the air-raid siren, I am so startled I act with complete calm, leaping up the stairs, two by two. The piercing wails rise and fall. Somewhere out there, hundreds of miles away, a soldier pushed a button launching an eight-ton, huge, senseless missile, which, at this very moment, is hurtling above the desert toward us, gathering speed. The siren wavers, then swells up again, wilder than ever, terrorizing the nation. For a moment, I'm unable to subdue the specter of luminous yellow clouds and poisonous sticky vapors unleashed by a man-made Scud, suspended in the air in the sky above and floating downward to suck us into suffocation or madness, to shock us into another episode of useless violence.

The worst thing you can do is wait for the attacks in solitude, shut inside a sealed room, watching only your own anxiety unfold.

I grab a roll of brown tape, shut the door, and seal up the frame, checking that every millimeter is airtight. I cannot see the world outside. The shutters have been drawn; weather stripping lines the inside of the windows' wooden frames so that particles of poisonous chemicals, lethal gases, and bacteria cannot penetrate. Double layers of plastic have been sealed over the windows with thick brown shipping tape in case the glass shatters.

The thing that gets me is knowing that if I were photographing I wouldn't be afraid. I keep thinking about how disassociated photographers are from the experience they photograph. It's as if when you're part of the press corps, you're swept into another world, a pseudo-event of your own making.

From a shelf in the closet I take out my personal "protection kit," a hat-sized cardboard box containing a tube of gray powder (to decontaminate the skin from chemicals); an atropine auto-injector (to be jabbed into the thigh muscle in the case of nerve gas); four gauze application pads; and the black rubber gas mask that I slip over my head.

It is at this point that I call my mother. I'm not sure exactly why I want to call right then, as the siren howls and with my mask on. I suppose I want to share my experience. But she's already seeing the attack on television, so I find myself asking her what's happening since I can't see beyond the room and nothing has yet been reported on the radio. I don't get any answers. Instead, she just keeps saying, "I can't believe you're calling me while you're under attack." I'm laughing, fogging up the mask and making it difficult to breathe. I hang up the phone after she begins pleading with me to come home.

I shut my eyes. As a child, I had trouble falling asleep and would lie on my back still as a twig and wait for the bullfrogs to tranquilize me. Sometimes they sang country ballads in a chorus, other times they rocked me like a robed choir humming the gospel, lulling me into serenity late at night. Their rich, throaty voices would fill the dark space outside my bedroom window, gusting out harmonies. Then a rousing soloist would belt the air, his voice echoing up and down the canal like outlines of a thought, lying just beyond the rim of vision.

As many times as I walked the towpath beside the canal, searching along its rocky, moss-grown edges, I never once saw the bullfrogs. Once I asked Jim the fisherman why I couldn't find them, and he said that just because you didn't see something didn't mean it wasn't there. I liked the idea that something could appear invisible and still be so clearly heard.

I see now that the camera became my voice, my search for truth, a way to define myself. Photography was a way to step inside a world that I felt outside of, to compose the chaos that tumbled within. But perhaps chaos isn't supposed to be tamed, numbered, and filed like slides in sheets of little plastic squares in a three-ring binder.

I used to believe in the truth of photo-reportage, in its impartiality, but the global manipulation of visual information and shaping of public opinion—how the war is represented and reported to the world at large—distresses me. Though we are witness to America's absolute techno-military superiority, we never actually "see" Operation Desert Shield. The war itself is censored, despite CNN's nonstop, round-the-clock, on-site transmissions. Most frightening, while the images create an illusion of intimacy with the moment, I can't help but wonder if I am witnessing the end of independent media coverage, the triumph of image over reality.

The fear that grips me tonight is not only the danger of the Scud missile attack. If I want to break out of my solitude, I have to break out of my silence. What had been my sanctuary is now a cage. Tonight I shall begin to throw away this mask of mine and fly through the images of time, allow memory to open the way and flood me with the images I must grasp of the past, find the courage to face myself. I will walk away.

32

The Striptease, Take 2

(JUNE/JULY 1991)

It's been three and a half years since the intifada began when the *Washington Post* asks me again to photograph a three-part series on the Strip. I am reluctant to take on the assignment. Gaza is quiet. The intifada has more or less dried up and is off the front pages. The violent demonstrations and riots have withered away.

I decide to take the assignment because I want to see what has changed for the Strip's residents, though I know the assignment will not be easy. I'm overwhelmed by the antiquity of the place, by a living past too old to belong to our own time, yet too present to lie dormant as if past. I am unable to let go of an image I know I'd oversimplified, sacred and mad, of a time and place lost in the lives of those who have vanished and of those on each street corner. There is something I want to frame.

Which is why I am sitting opposite Habeeb, the Palestinian version of Don Corleone.

"You want what?" I can't believe my ears. "You've got to be kidding," I nearly explode.

He nods his head. "$1,700 for a week. That's with a fifty-dollar reduction."

His business, a sophisticated escort service, is but one of the many "media service companies" that has burgeoned since the intifada to help the foreign press travel into and through "the territories" of the Gaza Strip and the West Bank safely. In 1984, when I first moved here, you could go anywhere, whenever you wished. Habeeb is representative of how Palestinian society has changed. Having not picked up a camera in Gaza for nearly a year, I am shocked to learn that now the only camerapeople operating freely in Gaza are young Palestinian men from the refugee camps who have been furnished with Super 8 video cameras by the foreign television networks.

When these new local stringers aren't shooting footage for the TV stations, they "escort" foreign photojournalists, a business that has turned into a mafia network. You can't go anywhere without a Palestinian guide, so that what I choose to look at is no longer a question of how much I want to see, but what I will be allowed to see, a trade-off the foreign press corps seems to accept.

Habeeb is sure I need him, and with the *shabiba*, the internecine fighting, and the growth of Hamas, he has a point. He assumes a big name like the *Washington Post* will pay a steep price. He tells me he understands photographers' needs very well, having escorted journalists for *Time* magazine for a matter of months, not to mention *National Geographic*.

You are in the Middle East, I remind myself. Dicker. "How much will it cost to have an escort for four days?" I ask.

"A thousand dollars," he says casually.

I mention at this point that I've covered the Middle East for the last eight years and have lived in the West Bank for the last two years. I am not a newcomer to the region. And beyond that, I simply don't have the kind of budget for that. I want a breakdown of costs.

He doodles around with a silver pen, then shows me the figures he's written on his notepad.

Gaza: $150 per day x 4 days = $600

"That's for a local escort," he explains.

Car: 200 Israeli shekels, with driver x 4 = 800

"That amounts to another $400," he says. "Gas included."

Total Cost, 4 Days = $1000

"In other words," I say, "your services will cost me $250 a day." It's not that I have anything against these new entrepreneurs, but something in me resents the fact that I have to pay to do a story. I feel like I'm being manipulated.

I finally tell him the situation. "Look, I can't swing it. The *Post* has allotted me a budget of $300 only." I try to explain the difference between a freelance photographer who's on assignment and a staff journalist's unlimited expense account.

He finds this unbelievable, then doodles around some more with the silver pen.

"Okay, for you, a special deal." He shows me the new figures on his notepad.

Gaza: $125 per day x 4 days = $500

Car: 140 Israeli shekels, with driver x 4 = 560 ($233.33)

"$800 for four days, or $200 per. A favor," he says. "Gas included."

The entire Strip is only thirty miles from north to south and less than five miles wide.

"Can we skip the driver?" I ask. "I mean, what about an escort who has his own car?"

He explains that he doesn't recommend this. I'm starting to get panicked.

"Final offer," he says. "$150 a day with escort and car, no driver. You pay for gas."

I nod, reluctantly agreeing.

I've been so wrapped up in logistics that it is only in the middle of the night that I wake up in a cold sweat and realize I will be traveling back to an environment that still frightens me.

WEDNESDAY, JUNE 26:

Leave for Gaza. Hamas strike to protest against Jewish settlements and immigration means no cars are moving in Gaza except relief organizations. I hitch a ride with UNRWA. From Jerusalem, the trip takes approximately two hours.

Because of the strike, the streets are empty, the shops and restaurants closed. The sky glitters overhead, and for a moment I remember how easy it once was to impose order on appearance, make it firm.

There are only two "hotels" in Gaza: the Beach Club, owned and run by the United Nations (no journalists, Palestinians, or Israelis allowed), and Marna House, run by Alia. I have excluded from my list the recently re-opened Palm Beach Hotel, a new settlers' resort, that is being advertised by its new owners as an orthodox Club Med.

I've been invited to stay at the Beach Club as long as I keep a low pro-file. At seven dollars a night, breakfast included, with an extra five bucks for air-conditioning, it's a bargain. Most importantly, there's a bar where I can watch the sun set over the sea. Here it's possible to breathe more freely, but I am conscious always that I can't step beyond the compound on my own, past the security guards who stand watch twenty-four hours a day. Even if I could, the town is under curfew. Stillness presides like a conspicuous stranger.

I wonder if my room is bugged, knowing that it most likely is. I know most of the hotel rooms I've stayed in over the years have been bugged, and sometimes my room has been searched.

THURSDAY, JUNE 27:

Morning with UNRWA and food distribution, then meet up with Talal, my escort. We go to souk (women in mourning); military camp (it was here the intifada began, nearly four years ago); two schools.

The Unified Leadership has ordered a "quiet week," a euphemism for a pause in riots so everyone can study. This suits me perfectly, since my intent is to photograph the people in a setting no one ever sees, to show what it means to actually live in their world.

Dead quiet. Woman in kitchen. Kids playing. Martyrs' cemetery (nobody there). Gaza is a cage within a cage. Garbage. Stench. Scorched sand. Worker's market (T pulling out ID to prove he's Palestinian). Downtown, end-of-day Gaza traffic.

As far as I can tell, the afternoon's pix will end up in the trash bin.

FRIDAY, JUNE 28:

Labor market . . .

We are trying to maintain a delicate balance between soldiers and laborers, friendly but distant.

. . . Cruising in the car . . .

It's impossible to walk. Once the kids start gathering, the shabiba become suspicious and unpredictable. People here feel that after three years, the press has done nothing for them, a sign of their inability to take responsibility for their own fate (Allah's will syndrome).

. . . Gaza souk (get pelted w/fruits & vegs).

MONDAY, JULY 1:

Talal picks me up at checkpoint.

. . . Red Cross pix, coffee shop/idle men.

TUESDAY, JULY 2, 6 A.M.:

Even fishermen at sea cannot escape curfew. Those who fish at night must leave before sunset and cannot return until dawn's first light. Talal wants breakfast, then we have to wait for his friend. I'm frustrated. The whole point is to do early morning pictures at camp. Talal mentions how many people are "protecting me." My suspicion is that Talal is uncomfortable in the camps, which makes working with him disconcerting.

WEDNESDAY, JULY 3:

Scenes in Rafa. Khan Younis. Crippled guy. Paralyzed young man. Intifada stories.

THURSDAY, JULY 4:

Jabalia souk again. Food distribution. Sewage. Men playing dominoes. Gaza military court.

FRIDAY, JULY 5:

Bomb threat on settlers' road. Soldiers are waving and twirling clubs at me. "Have a nice day," they say. "Just not here."

SUNDAY, JULY 7:

I ship fifty-five rolls of film to the *Washington Post*, relieved that the worst is over. The *Post's* foreign department goes berserk about the amount of rolls they first have to develop, and even worse, then edit. Fortunately, I have just clipped a story from the *New York Times Magazine* on photographer Sebastiao Salgado ("The Eye of the Photojournalist"; June 9, 1991) in which it is reported that he "shoots an average of ten to twelve rolls a day." I photocopy the story, earmarking the specific paragraph, and send it in with my bill to offset any further comments.

The last word from the foreign desk is that they're extremely pleased with the pictures and will be publishing seventeen.

Epilogue

All photographs are accurate.
None of them is the truth.
—RICHARD AVEDON

33

The Old Man

(NOVEMBER 1994)

I am without my cameras, here to witness Arafat's return to Palestine. I'm not on assignment for any news organization and haven't been for some time. Instead, I've spent the last two years photographing the conditions and environment of Palestinian refugee children for UNICEF, examining how military occupation and armed conflict affect their everyday life and psychology. It is an issue that has been consistently pushed aside and treated as if it was taboo by the media, as well as by the international community.

As I wait outside the fence of the Palestine Hotel with the throngs of press on their cell phones, I'm thinking about King Hussein. Last month, I witnessed the fulfillment of the promise he had given to his grandfather, King Abdullah, with the signing of the peace treaty between Israel and Jordan, an event downplayed by the Western media.

A car approaches and suddenly I'm thrust aside by a TV cameraman. Through the crowd I watch as Arafat and his entourage careen through the gates of the hotel, his Mercedes leaning over like a sailboat, with bodyguards splayed across the car at varying angles as if this were Lebanon. Kalashnikovs point everywhere.

Inside the beachfront headquarters of the Palestinian National Authority, I'm escorted past the smoky anteroom into an even smokier inner sanctum where the stagnant scent of nicotine greets me, as do about thirty pairs of male eyes. Nearly everyone is armed. I do not see Arafat, but I know he's here. Someone offers me a seat, then a cigarette, then a cup of coffee or tea.

I watch a parade of well-dressed PLO bureaucrats, longtime aides, soldiers in camouflaged uniforms, and professional bodyguards entertain a crowd of Gaza politicians, West Bank personalities, international diplomats. I am the only foreign journalist, and though I've not spoken to Arafat for many years, I realize that I'm getting in, at least in part, because I'm known to him.

Since returning to the homeland, more than 850 requests for interviews with the chairman have poured in, I'm told by one of Arafat's spokesmen, who points to a three-drawer filing cabinet. Four more requests have come over the fax machine in the last hour, but they too will be filed. Arafat is avoiding the foreign press corps.

Whispering, "He wants to see you now," Abu Fayez ushers me through a short hallway into a small conference room. The "Old Man" is sitting at his desk at the head of an oval conference table, scrutinizing a stack of documents. The expression on his unmistakably strange and familiar face, utterly concentrated.

I take a seat across from Arafat's chief spokesman, Marwan Kanafani. Because I'm trusted, often I don't have to undergo any security checks, and today is no exception. Usually, though, I carry out my own security checks in my hotel room before I go to see Arafat or Hussein because of the fear that someone might have hidden an explosive in my camera bag, etc.

Ten minutes pass before the PLO chieftain finally puts down his red felt-tip pen and with a cursory glance says: "Proceed."

I give a quick synopsis of a book I'm writing about the making of images in the Middle East, explaining that it will cover the period from 1984 to 1994—and since the chairman is one of my subjects, I thought the book would benefit from his viewpoint.

He doesn't say a word.

Slightly discouraged, I add that I would like to interview Arafat about the numerous media images he has both embodied, and been the victim of, over the last decade.

"But you're a photographer, aren't you?" asks Kanafani.

"Yes," I admit, explaining that my book is not about "current events," or "personalities," but rather about how we perceive them. It is the true story of a photojournalist who changes her views over time and experience, and as a result, is slowly compelled to set aside her cameras and reexamine the way images are created, scenes are framed, and how "real life" is packaged for specific news stories.

Arafat is unusually quiet, I suspect because in the five months since establishing residence in Gaza, the sixty-five-year-old Nobel laureate, who for thirty years symbolized Palestinian dreams and desires, has been recast by the Western press from a demigod into a despot.

People in the news business like to create images, as recent headlines I'd been collecting demonstrate: "For Palestinians in Gaza, There's a New Foe: Arafat"; "Gaza's Cry: 'Uprising Against Arafat Has Just Begun'"; "Who Can Save Arafat?"; "The Palestinians' Winter of Discontent with Arafat"; "Oslo Deal Left Gaza Trapped, Arafat Humiliated: Hawks Circle as Hopes Fade"; "The PLO Chief's Fall from Grace."

The images themselves—in this case, of Arafat's imminent demise—shape our perceptions of the Middle East. Their very purpose is to make people believe. But to what end?

The PLO chief listens to me intently and then asks one question: "Have you interviewed any other heads of state?"

"Yes," I reply.

"Who?" he wants to know.

"King Hussein."

"You've already interviewed him?"

"Yes. Many times," I acknowledge, fretting inwardly about how this elusive, enigmatic world figure will now react, given his longtime rivalry with the Jordanian monarch.

For a minute or two, he's silent.

"Okay," he says, "I will do it."

———

When the gates close I walk away, and I know that I am literally walking away from the foreign press corps. I know that I don't belong to this age of nonstop media-tech imagery, of "our camera-mediated knowledge," as Susan Sontag writes. This kind of life, this way of seeing, is no longer part of me, of who I am and who I want to be.

It is for this reason that I find myself writing, hesitantly at first, afraid of the lacunae in between images, the space between my photographs and myself. Habitually I save telexes, stuffing them after each assignment in marked and coded manila envelopes, figuring that one day they may be useful. It's an obsession, really. Remnants of press corps rap. An insider's guide to the cryptic world of professional journalism. A personal anthology. Evidence. I search through the piles of notes, articles, photographs, journals, and the various correspondences I've had with editors and colleagues—the fragments I've accumulated and saved after each assignment, wondering if one day these bits and pieces might be used to bring together a version of reality that remains largely unseen and overlooked. A complete story.

34

War on Another Front

— ELLEN SPENCER SUSMAN
(2007)

Carol's decision to write this book about her life and work in the Middle East began after she walked away from that November 1994 meeting with Yasser Arafat.

Earlier that year she had married Brian Mitchell, an Australian she met in Jerusalem. Brian was then the acting director of the United Nations Relief and Work Agency, West Bank. For the first time in many years, my sister was really at home.

Carol was a pack rat, an indefatigable researcher, and a meticulous writer. She labored over what she wrote and would redo chapters numerous times, often changing only a few words. One of the reasons the book took so long to complete was that Carol continued to develop her theme about how the media frame the issues. As she explained to Arafat, she wanted to write about how her views had changed over time and through experience. She felt strongly that judgment and truth had disappeared from news coverage, and that the version of reality visible to the viewer had no bearing on the reality of the situation.

In the end, she felt that the power of the pen was stronger than the "picture worth a thousand words."

So, Carol worked on *Danger Pay*, and received two book contracts. Each time, she decided she had not delved deeply enough into the philosophical theories about media usage, and canceled the contract in order to go to another level.

Besides putting down her cameras, Carol's life was changing in other ways. On New Year's Eve 1995, she delivered her only child in the Hadassah Hospital on the Mount of Olives. She named him Samuel, which means "God listens." After Sam's birth, my formerly fearless sister changed.

She simply wanted to be with her son, and she was a terrific mother. Her world centered around writing and Sam.

In 1998 Carol and her family came to Florida for the removal of a lump on her thyroid, called Hashimoto's Syndrome. After they returned to Israel, they decided it was time to move back to the United States. However, it took three years before the United Nations reassigned Brian to New York. They finally settled into a house in Croton-on-Hudson, New York, about two weeks before September 11, 2001. Carol wryly told me, "I thought we'd left this behind."

One year later, she was diagnosed with Stage 4 breast cancer, which she called "war on another front." She received wonderful treatment from Memorial Sloan-Kettering Hospital in New York City and struggled valiantly with the disease. She continued working on the book, which gave her focus and purpose during the last few months of her life. She passed away on April 15, 2004, just two weeks after her fiftieth birthday.

People ask why I took on the task of finishing Carol's book. First of all, she asked me to. Secondly, I wanted Sam, who was eight years old when she passed away, to remember his mom. And, I felt that her story needed to be told.

I hope there are young people with a passion for history and truth whom Carol will inspire.

I hope that her "behind the scenes" stories remind people that what we read and see in the news about the Middle East and terrorism is only a small part of a very long and complicated story.

And lastly, I wanted to know my sister. It wasn't until I read her words and stories that I finally understood her life. A lone woman, traveling in countries where women often were not welcome, lugging her cameras in the days before our now-instant communications, relying on herself. Like all true pioneers, she did it for love. And so did I.